As the retired Curator of the Carisbrooke Castle Museum, Roy Brinton is an acknowledged authority on the history of the Isle of Wight. He was born on the Island in East Cowes, and educated in Whippingham and Ryde, later joining the local history staff on the Isle of Wight County Council. He is well-known for his lectures on the Ryde area, and as the author of several books on old Isle of Wight illustrations, amongst them *Edwardian Island* (1992), *Victorian Island* (1994) and *Isle of Wight Century 1900-1999* (1999). He has recently been made Honorary President of Ryde Social Heritage Group.

FOLLOWING PAGES
Newtown Creek, the Quay.

ROY BRINTON
ISLE OF WIGHT
The Complete Guide

THE DOVECOTE PRESS

To all Islanders and 'Overners' who love this Island.

'The Isle of Wight has very numerous advantages to recommend it as a most agreeable spot to reside in: no place is happier in the beauties of a varied country: here are hills, dales, mountains, rocks, wood and water, all in perfection: a sea-coast that has not a perch of flat land; it all rises boldly from the water: they scarcely know what a marsh is. The land is admirably fertile in both grass and corn; game, particularly pheasants, in the greatest plenty: all provisions good, and surrounded by a sea, full of the finest fish in Britain. That it is healthy cannot be doubted, from the singularly happy circumstance of not a physician being there.'

ARTHUR YOUNG, 1771

Cowes Castle.

First published in 2006 by
The Dovecote Press Ltd
Stanbridge, Wimborne Minster,
Dorset BH21 4JD

Hardback   ISBN 1 904349 43 9
Paperback   ISBN 1 904349 42 0

Text © Roy Brinton 2006
Photographs © 2006 Roy Brinton,
Don French, David Yendall, Jack and
Johanna Jones, A.F. Kersting, Roger
Clark, Brading Roman Villa, The
British Museum, © Crown Copyright.
NMR, English Heritage.NMR, English
Heritage Photographic Library, GKN
Aerospace, Isle of Wight Museum
Services, Isle of Wight Bus Museum,
Lord Mottistone, Martin Munt, The
National Portrait Gallery, London,
Simmons Aerofilms Ltd, the University
of Bradford, Colin Varndell, and as
listed in the detailed Acknowledgements
on page 127.

The colour map is © Crown
Copyright. Cartography by Philip's.
© Philip's, an imprint of the Octopus
Publishing Group Ltd, 2006

Designed by The Dovecote Press
Printed and bound in Singapore

All papers used by The Dovecote Press
are natural, recyclable products made
from wood grown in sustainable, well-
managed forests

A CIP catalogue record for this book is
available from the British Library

Contents

The main MAP *and six pages of colour plates fall between pages 64 and 65*

Using this Book

The map in the centre of the colour section shows virtually all the places which have an entry in the alphabetical Gazetteer. The letter bracketed after each entry gives the relevant square in which it can be found on the map. In addition each of the towns has its own map, showing places of interest and car parks.

The lists at the back of the book give opening times and other information including a guide to those places which charge for admission (indicated by 'fee').

The 'must' list below suggests places to visit or enjoy for those staying for a short break. They are not necessarily the 'best', but they do give a real sense of the character and atmosphere of the Island, and some are of considerable historic importance.

Towns: Ryde; Ventnor; Yarmouth.

Archaeology: Roman villa, Brading.

Houses: Osborne; Arreton Manor; Appuldurcombe House (Wroxall).

Gardens: Ventnor Botanic Garden; Osborne House; Rylstone Gardens at Shanklin.

TOP *The Oglander Chapel, Brading Church.*
ABOVE *Brading, a mosaic from the Roman villa.*
BELOW *Carisbrooke Castle.*

Villages: Bonchurch; Brading; Brighstone; Niton; St Helens; Shorwell; Godshill.

Churches (medieval): Arreton; Shalfleet; Bonchurch; Brading; Godshill.

Churches (19th century): All Saints (Ryde); Whippingham; St Thomas (Newport).

Museums: Carisbrooke Castle; Museum of Island Life, Guildhall (Newport); Dinosaur Isle (Sandown).

Other: Newtown area; Calbourne Water Mill; Carisbrooke Castle; Amazon World Zoo Park (Arreton); Shanklin Chine.

Walks: High Down, Freshwater; Newtown area; Medina Valley; Parkhurst Forest; Culver Down; Brading Down.

Maps

For those who will be mainly using the car the Ordnance Survey Landranger Map No. 196 (1:50,000) is suitable as it shows both the A and B class roads and covers the whole of the Island.

For those who will be doing some exploring on foot the Ordnance Survey Explorer Map No. OL 29 (1:25,000) is needed as it shows the field boundaries, as well as all footpaths and bridleways.

Both of these maps are available at the Tourist Information Centres and most bookshops.

ABOVE *Cottages in Shorwell.*
BELOW *Dinosaur Isle Museum, Sandown.*

England in Miniature

The Isle of Wight is England in miniature. Somewhere on the Island you will find an example of the mainland's landscape. There are over 60 miles of varied coastline – high cliffs, sheltered coves, marshes and seaside towns with sandy beaches. Inland there are high downs, woodlands, picturesque villages, river valleys and miles of open farmland.

The main ridge of downland across the Island, from east to west, forms a natural division between north and south. The northern half has heavy soils and contains much of the woodland, such as Hamstead, Parkhurst Forest and Combley Great Wood. The fields tend to be small and the hedgerows rich in trees.

To the south of the downs is a large open fertile plain with panoramic views from Sandown Bay, across the Island to the south west coast. The plain is the Island's best farmland, yielding crops ranging from wheat and early potatoes to garlic, or salad crops grown under glass. Its southern boundary is edged by the high downs of St Boniface and St Catherine.

The high quality of the landscape has warranted the designation of over half the Island as an Area of Outstanding Natural Beauty. The mainland may only be a short boat ride away, but the atmosphere on the Island is quite different. With a mild climate, sunshine records and a slightly slower pace of life, it is easy to relax. There is time and space for all to enjoy their stay, no matter what their tastes may be.

A good way to discover the western end of the Island is on the open-top bus which goes from Yarmouth to the Old Needles Battery. Alum Bay is on the left.

Gazetteer

ADGESTONE (G)

The two country lanes from Brading to Alverstone both pass through this small hamlet. It consists of two farms, a few cottages and a row of modern houses. The hamlet nestles under Brading Down and faces south.

This makes it ideal for the Adgestone Vineyard, whose winery, gift shop and café are in Upper Adgestone Road. Although the vines were only planted in 1968, the vineyard is thought to be one of the oldest in England, and may well have been first planted by the Romans. Adgestone Vineyard wines were given to the Queen in 1994 at a dinner to celebrate the 50th anniversary of the Normandy Landings.

This is a pleasant rural area to drive and walk through, and there are several footpaths leading off the roads.

ALUM BAY (D)

One of the Isle of Wight's most popular places, the Bay lies at the extreme western end of the Island. For hundreds of years it has been famed for its cliffs, which boast around 20 different shades of coloured sands. The Victorians used the sands to create pictures of Island scenes, which are displayed in local museums and are now collectable. The best way to see this remarkable natural phenomenon is to use the chair lift, which runs between the cliff top and the beach. On the cliff edge there is a memorial to Guglielmo Marconi (1874-1937), who set up the first permanent wireless station in the world here in 1897.

The principal tourist attraction at Alum Bay is the Needles Pleasure Park, whose activities include glass blowing, sweet making and emulating the tourists of more than a century ago by creating a picture using coloured sands.

From the Pleasure Park there is an

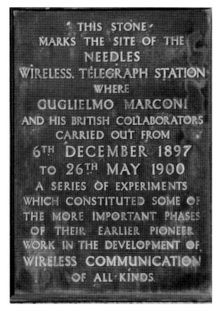

ABOVE *Alum Bay. The monument marking the site of the hotel were Marconi stayed and carried out his wireless experiments in 1897.*

BELOW *Alum Bay. Using the coloured sands to fill glass jars with attractive designs at the Needles Pleasure Park.*

open-top bus service up to the Old Needles Battery, which was built in 1861-63 to defend the narrow Needles Channel, the stretch of water between the Island and Hurst Castle on the mainland, from attack by the French. The Battery is now in the ownership of the National Trust and is open in the summer. Apart from the obvious interest of the building it gives wonderfully dramatic views of the Needles.

From the cliffs there is a fine walk east, along High Down towards the Monument to the poet Alfred, Lord Tennyson, and on to Freshwater Bay.

ALVERSTONE (F)

Quiet and peaceful and well away from main roads, the village's secluded development in the 19th century is largely explained by the purchase of several farms by Thomas Webster. When his son Richard, a barrister, MP for the Isle of Wight, and later Lord

Alverstone. Cottage showing the arms (on the wall below the chimney stack) of the Webster family.

ABOVE & LEFT *Alverstone. Two of the original 1930s houses in Alverstone Garden Village. The one above, The Lodge, was the first house to be built and the date stone of 1923 visible under the right hand window and placed there at the opening ceremony still survives.*

Chief Justice and Viscount Alverstone (1842-1915), bought additional land in the area, the Alverstone Estate was formed. Several cottages in the centre of the village bear the cipher of the Webster family and date stones.

The school has now become the village hall and there are a number of helpful maps outside to assist the visitor. One shows the location of Alverstone Mead, once farmed as water meadows. It is now a 44 acre nature reserve comprising wetland, ancient woodland, meadows and ditches, with particularly good wetland flowers and dragonflies.

To the south west is Alverstone Garden Village. In the early 1920s a group of local businessmen purchased Youngwoods Copse and offered building plots to those who wished to live in a new rural development. The copse was cleared, leaving only the mature trees. A new road, Youngwoods Drive, was formed, running north to south through the estate and connected to the highway at each end. The plans were that over 100 houses and bungalows would be built in the countryside, plus a village hall, tennis courts and pleasure grounds. The speculators hoped to attract the professional classes to purchase plots.

The first bungalow was erected early in 1923, and in October the Island's M.P., Sir Edgar Chatfield-Clarke, declared the village open and unveiled a stone on the front wall of the bungalow. Take up of plots was slow and by 1926 only 10 houses had been built,

increasing to 17 by 1933. Possible reasons include poor communications, the lack of electricity and any shops. Residents had to rely on tradesmen from Sandown and Shanklin to call for orders.

It was not until car ownership became popular that the Garden Village began to grow, and in the 1970s builders were offering to erect a range of houses and bungalows at prices from £18,500 for a two bedroom bungalow, to £25,500 for a four bedroom house. Today Youngwoods Drive (now Youngwoods Way) is full and further roads have had to be constructed to meet the demand of those who wish to live in well-wooded countryside.

At the bottom of the hill, on the road to Alverstone, flows the river Eastern Yar, which has a number of attractive walks along its banks. Another excellent walk is up the Foxes Hole Lane to the top of the Downs. The views across the valley are splendid.

APSE HEATH (F)

The hamlet straddles a crossroads on the main Sandown to Newport Road. It has a post office and a shop, which serve the area to the north including Winford. Towards Sandown is the stone-built Methodist chapel dated 1902. Its predecessor, of 1875, is next door and now serves as a church hall.

ARRETON (F)

The village nestles in the sheltered valley to the south of Arreton Down. Stretching for more than two miles along the main road to Sandown this elongated and straggling village ends at the Fighting Cocks Inn. The view looking down from the downs clearly shows the surrounding fields that help restrict any increase in housing. When viewed from the south the village is seen against the backdrop of the chalk downland.

The heart of the village is at Arreton Cross Roads where lie the Church of St George and the village school. The church stands behind the White Lion Inn and has been a place of worship for

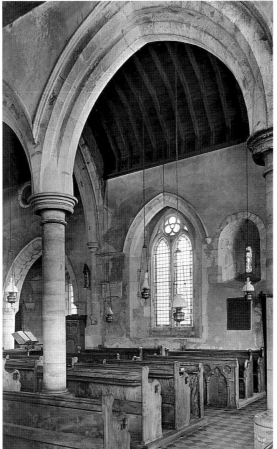

ABOVE *Arreton, the Church of St George, with two massive buttresses supporting the tower.*

LEFT *The interior when still lit by oil lamps.*

FAR LEFT *The 15th century brass of Henry Hawls, who fought under Henry V at the Battle of Agincourt in 1415.*

more than a thousand years. The present building dates from the 11th century – when it came under the care of Quarr Abbey – and is well worth a visit, especially to see the Saxon work. The west wall is largely Saxon, with its original doorway, now abutted by a later tower. Part of the north wall of the chancel also contains Saxon fabric. The huge buttresses supporting the tower were added after the steeple was struck by lightning in about 1500.

Other notable features are an early 15th century brass to Henry Hawls, a veteran of Agincourt and 'Long tyme steward of the Yle of Wyght', the Baroque monuments of the Worsley Holmes family, and the 1992 Burma Star Memorial window, designed by Alan Younger.

Arreton. The grave of Elizabeth Wallbridge, a housemaid made famous by a religious tract.

19th and early 20th centuries it was used mainly as a farmhouse, but later in the 20th century it was restored and is now open to the public. It is worth visiting to see the finely carved panelling in the main room.

Between the church and the manor house is Arreton Barns Craft Village, which is housed in a mixture of old, and new buildings. Glass making, pottery and woodcrafts are all demonstrated here. There is also a tea room, and extensive gift shop. Here also is Jacob's Yard, which in the Shipwreck Centre contains an absorbing collection of exhibits including coins recovered from the seabed, tales of diving operations and lifeboat rescues.

The rest of the village stretches along the busy road and there is a mixture of old thatched cottages, 19th century brick built houses and two 20th century closes of modern houses, erected mainly on the north side of the road with their backs to the Downs. Near the end of the village is the Methodist chapel, built in 1879, with an earlier chapel – now used as a schoolroom – alongside.

Still further along is the lane (right of way) to Heasley Manor House which is privately owned, but can be seen from the lane. The west wing is the oldest part, dating from 1538. The south wing dates from early the following century and the small north wing was added

Arreton. Bronze Age daggers and axeheads from the Arreton Hoard.

about a hundred years later. The manor was a grange belonging to Quarr Abbey until the Dissolution of the Monasteries. The manor passed to John Mill of Southampton, and later his grand-daughter Douzabelle Paulet, who regularly entertained Sir Edward Horsey, Governor of the Isle of Wight between 1565 and 1582. Sir Edward probably shared Douzabelle's bed as well as her hospitality, and there is a fine monument to him in St Thomas's Church, Newport. The house later passed to Sir Thomas Fleming, an Islander who was a judge at the 1606 trial of the Gunpowder Plotters, and remained in the Fleming family for nearly 350 years.

Arreton is surrounded by well-drained fertile soil, which has proved excellent for horticulture and the large scale growing of salad crops. Sweetcorn and garlic are also grown extensively in the valley. There is a range of footpaths providing a number of easy walks. On the Down above the village is Robin Hill Country Park, which has activities for all ages.

In the late 18th century two farmers found a cache of Bronze Age (approximately 2000 BC) objects buried in the chalk on Arreton Down. What became known as the Arreton Hoard consisted of two of the earliest spearheads found in Great Britain and several daggers and axes. It is thought they were buried by Bronze Age smiths and traders, to be collected at a later date. Today the hoard is in the British Museum.

In the churchyard is the grave of Elizabeth Wallbridge (d. 1801), a housemaid who found posthumous fame as the heroine of Leigh Richmond's tract *The Dairyman's Daughter*, and the brick tomb of Cromwell's grandson, William, and his wife.

Nearby is the manor house, a stone H-plan structure. In the centre of the front elevation is a porch with the date 1639, which was when the house was rebuilt for Sir Humphrey Bennett. In the

Arreton. The east front of the manor house.

Ashey. The seamark of 1735, built on the site of an old windmill.

Bembridge. The old 1920s telephone box.

ASHEY (F)

More descriptive of an area rather than a village or hamlet, Ashey lies at the foot of the north side of Ashey Down. There is one group of houses in Station Road, which leads to the halt on the Isle of Wight Steam Railway line from Havenstreet to Smallbrook interchange.

The only other area of housing is around East Ashey Farm, on the site of the manor house. The area has a long history and once was a wealthy manor, which stretched as far as Ryde.

Only a few yards from the house stood the now lost village of Ashey, a deserted 15th century medieval village. It was probably abandoned because of fear of raiders from across the Channel, and there is nothing to be seen above ground. To the west is West Ashey Farm, which was established as a model farm in the mid 19th century.

Lovely walks in this area include one from the railway halt to the top of Ashey Down, the reward for the climb being some magnificent views across the Solent. On the summit a seamark of 1735 shows where a naval semaphore station once signalled shipping movements off the Island to Portsmouth Naval Dockyard.

BEMBRIDGE (G)

At the beginning of the 19th century Bembridge was a small village dependent on living by fishing and victualling ships at anchor offshore.

Expansion initially began in 1825 when Edward Wise inherited a considerable estate and provided the incentive for building Regency villas in the area around the church (1827) – and where church, school (now the library) and vicarage remain grouped together. As Bembridge grew more fashionable, roads were widened. In 1829 a ferry to St Helens was started. Then came a steady growth of new roads and houses. Finally an embankment was built to carry the road and the railway line from St Helens to Bembridge. When the embankment was completed in 1882, Brading Harbour was drained and most of the reclaimed land used for the grazing of cattle.

To the north of the embankment lies the present Bembridge Harbour, which as well as providing a refuge for a number of houseboats also contains the headquarters of the Bembridge Sailing Club, well-known for its Redwing yachts with their instantly recognisable, brightly-coloured sails.

The most attractive way to approach the village is via Embankment Road from St Helens, passing the 1930s Pilot

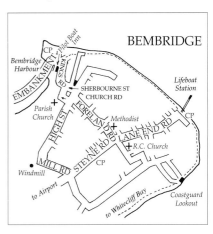

Boat Inn, which is built in the shape of a ship's bow.

In the High Street is a 1920s telephone box, which is believed to be the oldest K1 type still in daily use in Britain.

The High Street and Foreland Road contain a bank, shops and restaurants, and there are more shops in Lane End Road.

At the north end of Lane End Road is the lifeboat station, first established in 1867. The modern boathouse is at the end of the pier and the lifeboat is launched down a ramp. The station is occasionally open to the public. The original lifeboat station is still standing at the shore end of the pier and is now used for the inshore boat. The *Jessie Lumb* is the lifeboat best remembered

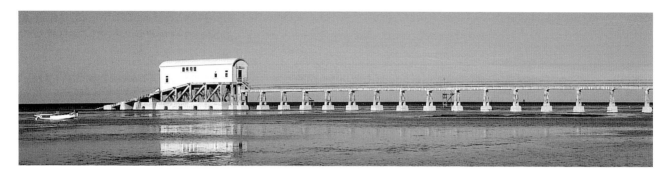

ABOVE *Bembridge. The Lifeboat Station.*

RIGHT *Bembridge. The Island's only surviving windmill stopped grinding corn in 1913. It was a lookout during the Second World War and now belongs to the National Trust.*

locally. She came, brand new, in 1939 and served throughout the Second World War, rescuing airmen from aircraft that had come down in the sea as well as sailors and victims of shipwrecks. Between 1939 and her final retirement in 1970 the *Jessie Lumb* was launched 294 times and saved 280 lives.

Out to sea to the east is the Nab Tower, which sits on a rock on the edge of the Bembridge Ledge. The concrete and steel structure was built at Shoreham, Sussex, towards the end of the First World War, and was intended to be one of a chain of towers placed across the English Channel to stop German submarines reaching the Atlantic. The war ended with only one tower complete, so Trinity House decided to use it instead of the lightship. It was towed into place after the war, and owes its slight tilt to not being dropped squarely when finally released. Today the tower is unmanned and the light is fully automated.

The parish church of Holy Trinity was erected in 1847 near the site of an earlier building, which was built just 20 years earlier but was demolished after becoming unsafe. The interior is light and airy and there are attractive stained glass windows. The organ was installed

Bembridge. The 1920s Arts and Crafts interior of the chapel at the former Bembridge School.

in 1887 to mark Queen Victoria's Golden Jubilee, and was first played by Mr Seadden, the Queen's organist.

The present Methodist chapel in Foreland was built in 1934 and is the third one in the village. The earlier building erected in 1844 can still be seen in King's Road but is now a private house. When the Methodists moved out, it became the Roman Catholic church, giving them a permanent home after they had been forced to make do with a variety of temporary accommodation, including a disused railway carriage and a garage. The Catholics moved into a new and much larger church in 1965.

On the corner of the High Street and Mill Road is the Island's only surviving windmill. Built in the 18th century it was used to grind corn and animal food. The mill ceased to be used in 1913. In the 1930s some restoration work was done. During the Second World War it served as an H.Q. and lookout for the Army and the Home Guard. The mill was given to the National Trust in 1958, who carried out repairs and restoration work. The inside contains

all the milling machinery and is a fascinating place to visit. Open to the public during the summer.

On the cliff face between Bembridge and Whitecliff Bay is a group of buildings which were once the well-known Bembridge School, founded in 1919 by the educationalist J. Howard Whitehouse, who believed creative education was as important as academic work. He was Warden of the school until his death in 1955 at the age of 82. In the 1920s he commissioned a series of buildings for the School by the Arts and Crafts architect M.H. Baillie Scott, which still survive today. The school closed 1996-97 and is now a boarding campus and an educational study centre: little can be seen from the road.

To the south of Bembridge is Whitecliff Bay, whose attractive sandy beach is flanked on the south side by the towering cliffs of Culver Down. There is a large caravan holiday park at Whitecliff Bay, which is private, but there is a public path from the road down to the beach. Out to sea stretches the Bembridge Ledge, a shallow ledge of limestone and the cause of many shipwrecks.

On the Down above the bay is Bembridge Fort, built 1862-67 as part of the extensive defence system to guard Portsmouth from possible invasion by the French. It was acquired by the National Trust in 1967, but it is not open to the public at present.

On the road from Bembridge to Brading is Bembridge Airport. It boasts the only concrete runway on the Island, and was laid out on land originally reclaimed from Brading Haven. Adjacent is the aircraft works which build the 'Islander' aircraft, which are in service all over the world. A further memorial to the 'Islander' can be found near the north-east corner of Bembridge churchyard, where a headstone incorporating an engraving of the plane commemorates John Britten (d. 1977), who with Desmond Norman designed and built it.

Whitecliff Bay from Culver Down.

BINSTEAD (B)

Although it is now part of Ryde and divided by the main Ryde to Newport road, Binstead is still regarded as a village. It is also home to several notable historic sites. To the north of the main road are the quiet lanes that lead to the ancient church and the stone quarries. The quarries – the last of which closed in the mid 19th century – are said to have been opened by the Romans. The Normans thought so highly of Quarr limestone from Binstead that it was exported for buildings on the mainland, including Winchester and Chichester cathedrals, and Southampton's town walls. Quarr stone was used to build the local medieval abbey (*see below*).

The parish church of Holy Cross retains its late 13th century chancel despite later alterations and rebuilding.

A Norman doorway has been re-erected in the churchyard. The keystone incorporates the weathered stone carving of what is probably a symbol of fertility, or sheela-na-gig, and is known locally as the Idol. Near the south-east corner of the church is the gravestone of Thomas Sivell, a smuggler 'cruelly shot on board his sloop' in 1785 by revenue officers.

There is a fine walk westwards from the church to the ruins of Quarr Abbey, the great Cistercian abbey founded in 1132 by Baldwin de Redvers, the Lord of the Island (died 1155), some of whose bones may have been those found in a grave in the north wall of the abbey church. Although a site further inland would have been more fertile, it seems probable that the Abbey was built close to the sea because it owned

Binstead. The ruins of the first Quarr Abbey, built in the 12th century.

Binstead. Quarr Abbey showing the west end of the church built 1911-12.

ships based at Fishbourne. Over the years the Abbey acquired considerable estates, including a water mill at Wootton Bridge and a large grange at Haseley (*see* Arreton). The Abbey closed in 1536 following the Dissolution of the Monasteries. The grounds were sold by the Crown. The new owners stripped the buildings, and much of the stone was re-used by Henry VIII to build his Solent forts.

Just beyond the old abbey, is the modern abbey of Quarr, built in 1908 for a community of Benedectine monks who had left Normandy during a period of religious persecution. The distinctive buildings are of Flemish brick. The original design was inspired by Spanish architecture, and the architect, a Benedictine monk called Paul Bellot, is considered to be 'one of the pioneers of 20th century expressionism' (Nikolaus Pevsner). Quarr Abbey is Bellot's principal work. The interior of the Abbey church is extraordinary and is one of the Island's architectural highlights. All visitors are welcome to

Quarr Abbey, the nave; austere yet beautiful.

St Catherine's Oratory on the Down above Blackgang.

enter the church and to enjoy the gardens and the café.

There is another lovely walk, south from the ruins of the old abbey through Puckers Copse to Newnham Farm. To the left of the copse are the fishponds of the old abbey.

BLACKGANG (I)

Wonderful views of the so-called Back of the Wight, and indeed across much of the Island, are the reward for those climbing the short but steep path from the car park alongside the Blackgang Road to the top of St Catherine's Down. On top of this southerly point is St Catherine's Oratory, which despite looking like a medieval prototype for a space rocket is all that remains of an oratory built in the early 14th century. A resident priest would climb the tower and ensure a light was burning to guide the shipping off the coast.

Over the years much of the hamlet of Blackgang has fallen into the sea and little survives. What does remain, however, are the sooty black cliffs that gave it a name and the Chine – a deep narrow cut made in the soft rock by a stream.

Today, thousands of visitors come to the Chine to enjoy the attractions on offer at Blackgang Chine Fantasy Theme Park, a forty acre clifftop site. Alexander Dabell came to the Island in the 1820s to work at a Newport lace-making mill, but he had the instincts of

an entrepreneur and a showman's flair for publicity. In 1843 he obtained the old 'gang', or gangway down to the beach used by fishermen and smugglers.

The Island was fast becoming a holiday resort and Dabell made paths down the Chine to the beach (now closed). He obtained an 80-ton whale floating dead off the coast and had its skeleton put on display. It can still be

The entrance to the Blackgang Chine Fantasy Theme Park.

Looking west from above Blackgang Chine Fantasy Theme Park along the Back of the Wight.

seen today. In the following year he published a guide book showing an hotel at the head of the Chine. The number of attractions has continued to grow – likewise the number of visitors. Over the years there have been several landslips and the Dabell family, who still own the Park, have had to move their various attractions further inland. Today the Park's amusements include Pirate Fort, Cowboy Town, Dinosaurland and Fairy Castle.

To the east of the Chine, and starting from the car park on the main road above Blackgang, is a cliff-top walk, which follows the southern-most tip of the Island. There are impressive views over the old road to Niton, which was blocked by a large landslip in 1928, and on out to sea. The path ends at the western end of Niton village.

BLACKWATER (F)

Near Blackwater Cross, the junction of the Newport-Sandown and Newport-Shanklin roads, lies a collection of modern houses known as Blackwater. Here, the River Medina, a mere stream at this point – flows towards Newport Harbour. Between the hamlet and Blackwater Corner is the former railway station. A walk along Sandy Lane brings you to Whitecroft, until recently the Island's mental hospital, whose distinctive tower is visible throughout the valley.

To the east of the small hamlet is St George's Down. Early in the 17th century the Governor of the Island, the 3rd Earl of Southampton, had a bowling green laid out on the summit for the gentry. The area is now the home of Newport Golf Course.

The cycle track from Newport to Sandown, which passes through Blackwater, offers some interesting walks and safe cycling either to Merstone and on to Sandown, or in the opposite direction into Newport.

BONCHURCH (J)

Today it seems like a rural extension of Ventnor, but the beautiful village of Bonchurch has a fascinating and much longer history than its upstart neighbour. It was initially famed for its stone, which was quarried on the site of the present village until the 19th century.

The Old Church of St Boniface, at the eastern end of the village, is well worth a visit, especially in spring when the churchyard is full of daffodils and primroses. The present building dates from the 13th century, although a church is recorded on the site in the Domesday Book. The interior is plain, only a simple arch dividing nave and chancel. Charles I, when imprisoned at Carisbrooke, attended the funeral of Sir Ralph Chamberlayne in the church. On the walls are memorials to the Hill family, who were local landowners. Candle-lit services are held on Sunday evenings in the summer months.

In the early 19th century the scenery and mild climate, plus the bracing sea air, attracted Victorians visitors to the village, which is sheltered from the north by St Boniface Down. Doctors recommended the area for those suffering from poor health.

The Rev. James White, retired and living in Bonchurch, wrote to his friend

Bonchurch. The old Church of St Boniface.

Bonchurch. The village hall.

Charles Dickens with glowing accounts of the Isle of Wight. This prompted Dickens to bring his family to Bonchurch in July 1849 and to take a property called 'Winterbourne' for the summer (it is still possible to see the house from the churchyard of the Old Church). Whilst staying in Bonchurch Dickens amused himself with frequent expeditions to the top of St Boniface Down and along the coast. He also described long games of rounders on the beach with all of Bonchurch looking on. At Winterbourne he wrote several chapters of *David Copperfield*, and was visited by many of his literary friends including William Thackeray, Thomas Carlyle and Alfred Tennyson (*see also under* 'Writers and Poets').

From the coastal path to the east of the church there is a view, on the left, of East Dene, once the home of Admiral and Lady Swinburne. Their son was the poet Algernon Charles Swinburne, who was baptised in the old church in 1837 and brought up in the village. He died in 1909 and was buried at the new parish church of St Boniface.

The construction of a new church was begun in the 1840s when a rapidly expanding population meant that the old church was inadequate for the needs of the villagers. Built of local stone in 1847-48 and designed by the Victorian architect Benjamin Ferrey, it is on a level plot of land up the hill from East Dene. Inside, it is light and airy and, to the left

of the chancel, a screen forms a fine memorial to Admiral Jellicoe (1859-1935), famed for his exploits at the Battle of Jutland in 1916. Later created an earl, Jellicoe lived in retirement in nearby St Lawrence. More recently, some wonderfully colourful needle-work, stitched by a local artist Joan Wolfenden, and other villagers, have been added. These alone make the church an essential part of any visit to Bonchurch.

Beside the road in the centre of the village is the pond, a highly popular beauty spot. Formerly a withy bed, it was given to the village by Henry de Vere Stacpole (1861-1951), in memory of his wife who died in 1934. He was the author of the best selling *Blue Lagoon*, a tropical romance published in 1908 and more recently filmed (1980). The pond had been in the grounds of his house.

Bonchurch boasts narrow, winding lanes which lead down from the main road to the beach. At the bottom of Shore Road is Monk's Bay, where monks from the Abbey of Lyre in Normandy are supposed to have landed in 755. From here it is a short walk to the Esplanade and then on to Ventnor. In the right weather, this is a splendid route to choose.

BRADING (G)

Sited on the busy Ryde to Sandown road, Brading is one of the Island's most bustling villages. It has a long history going back to when the Romans probably had a port here. In the 16th century the sea came up to the backs of the houses in the High Street, but from 1562 embankments were raised and the land reclaimed, with only a lane (Quay Lane) giving access to a quay to the north of the village. There is plenty to offer to the tourist, walker or casual visitor. The best approach route is from the north, where the first landmark is the church on the left. This 12th century building is reputed to be the site of the first conversion of pagan Islanders to Christianity by St Wilfrid.

The church is entered under the west tower and processes towards the east end. Processional passages such as this are very rare, and are found in only two other English churches.

The interior of the church boasts a number of notable works of art, including, on the south wall, a large brass dedicated to the Rev Leigh Richmond, who was curate in charge here from 1797 to 1805 and author of

Brading. The Church of St Mary the Virgin from the east.

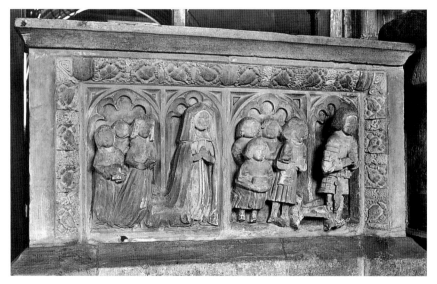

the famed *Annals of the Poor*, a bestseller in the early 19th century and published in several languages. Little Jane, one of the principal characters in the book, lived in the village and is buried in the churchyard. Her grave is marked with a tombstone near the east end of the church. In the north aisle, at the east end, is another notable memorial, this time to Elizabeth T.A. Rollo, who died in 1875, aged 15 months. It shows a little girl asleep on a mattress. The family had a house in Ryde.

Also inside the church is the Oglander Chapel, which contains some fine tombs of the local lords of the manor, including Oliver Oglander's (died 1536) stone alter tomb with its fine carving of Sir Oliver kneeling with his family. There are three wooden effigies of knights in the chapel. Medieval in style, they are not intended to represent the deceased, and at least one was installed by Sir John Oglander during his lifetime. The two largest are the tombs of Sir William (died 1609) and his son, Sir John himself (died 1655: the well known historian). The smaller effigy in the niche above is a memorial to Sir John's much-loved son, George, who died of smallpox aged 23.

In the northern part of the churchyard is the stone-built gun shed (restored in 1983), which once held the parish gun given to the village in the 16th century. At the south-east end of the burial ground is the cattle pound, also stone built, which was used to hold stray animals. Next to this building is a gate leading to Quay Lane. Before the land was reclaimed from the sea, this led to Brading Harbour.

Next door to the church is the old

TOP *Brading, the Church of St Mary the Virgin. The 16th century tomb of Oliver Oglander.*

CENTRE *Brading, the Church of St Mary the Virgin. The 17th century tomb of Sir John Oglander with a memorial to his son George in the niche above.*

LEFT *Brading. The old Town Hall which is said to date from the 16th century.*

ABOVE *Brading. The Bull Ring.*

RIGHT *Brading. The east front of Nunwell House, built in 1720.*

Town Hall, said to date from Elizabeth I, the ground floor of which can be seen through brick arches, which lead to the stocks, whipping post and the old village lock-up, which served as a small jail. The hall is on the first floor. The next building down the High Street is an early 16th-century timber-framed house, which is now home to The Brading Experience; a wax works with displays of historical events and figures as well as a chamber of horrors, a world of nature and a café. Almost directly opposite is the extremely popular Lilliput Doll and Toy Museum, loved by children of all ages. On the same side of the street, a little further along, is Brading Heritage Centre, which contains items of memorabilia and photographs of the village's past.

The High Street now climbs to reach the Bull Ring, an open area used up until the early 19th century for the baiting of bulls by dogs. The ring used is still visible. To one side of the Bull Ring is the new Town Hall, built in 1902, and opposite is The Mall, lined with houses in a range of different styles. The first on the left dates from the 17th century and is timber clad. On the other side is 'Beechgrove', a fine, late 17th century town house.

There are several places of interest close to Brading, the most notable of which is the Roman villa. Recently restored, the 3rd-century villa, once part of a prosperous farming estate, contains some of the finest Roman mosaics in England. The building is open all year

round and for seven days a week. Also nearby is Morton Manor, which has award-winning gardens.

To the east of the village, in Coach Lane, is Nunwell House, home of the Oglander family for more than 400 years. Prior to that the family lived at West Nunwell, but the house was burnt down and they moved to East Nunwell, site of the present house. The 17th-century house has had many alterations and additions and today consists of a Jacobean west wing connected to a Georgian east wing by a central hall. The south front was faced with mathematical tiles in 1700 and further additions have been made more recently.

The house is open to the public in the summer, and the suite of principal rooms, including the dining room, drawing room and library, contain fine furniture and paintings. At the top of the wooden staircase is the King's Room in which, in 1647, Charles I slept when visiting Sir John Oglander. Two rooms contain objects belonging to the Aylmer family, the present owners of the house, and in the cellar is the Home Guard Museum. On a fine day, there are six acres of garden to be enjoyed.

For hundreds of years the Oglander family have had a considerable influence on Island life. Sir John Oglander (1585-1655) was Deputy Governor of the Island and an historian who left us a wonderful account of life on the Island during the 17th century. Sir John was an ardent Royalist who endured imprisonment and heavy fines

for his friendship with Charles I. Sir William (1733-1806) took a great interest in everyday matters and was Chairman of the House of Industry – the workhouse – for 19 years. Major General Henry Oglander (1788-1840) fought in the Peninsular War (1808-14) where he lost an arm. He was also the first regimental commanding officer to abolish corporal punishment. John Henry Glynn Oglander (1847-1924) was a Fellow of the Society of Antiquaries and assisted the architect Percy Stone with his history of the Island, published at the end of the 19th century.

Brading is the starting point for a number of enjoyable walks, one of which begins in Quay Lane and continues across the marshes towards Bembridge. Alternatively, walk along The Mall and turn right by Little Jane's Cottage, walking up through the woods and on to Brading Down, which offers fine views west along the Arreton Valley and south to Shanklin.

Sir John Oglander.

Crossing to the Island

One of the joys of travelling to the Isle of Wight, given favourable weather, must be the journey across the Solent from the mainland. For the visitor, this boat trip heightens the sense of separateness that an island inhabitant may take for granted. For some not used to frequent sea travel, the ferry crossing is an adventure in itself. Certainly it can be the leisurely final stage of the journey, the true start of the holiday perhaps. This interlude encourages a sense of excitement and anticipation among visitors, particularly those landing on the Island for the first time.

The Solent is a sheltered stretch of water, benefiting from the protection of land to the north and south. Rarely, therefore, is the ferry crossing uncomfortably rough and there are few occasions in the year when ferries are cancelled because of poor weather conditions.

Although the journey from the mainland to the Island is relatively short there is always something of interest to see. There are naval ships and cross-Channel ferries leaving and entering Portsmouth Harbour, cruise ships and tankers in Southampton Water, as well as yachts, fishing boats and Isle of Wight ferries – making this one of the busiest stretches of water on the British coast. There are also the historic coastal defences and dockyard buildings to view.

To get an excellent overview of the Island before making the crossing, the recently completed 558 feet (170 metres) high Spinnaker Tower overlooking Portsmouth Harbour offers breathtaking views of the Island's north shore, from Bembridge in the east to the Needles in the west, and then inland to the central chalk ridge.

The times of the various crossings on offer vary from a leisurely one-hour trip, from Southampton to East/West Cowes by ferry, to ten minutes by hovercraft from Southsea to Ryde. Perhaps the most scenic route is via the ferry between Lymington and Yarmouth, especially on summer evenings when the sun is setting beyond the Needles. Today a frequent car and passenger service operates, with a journey time of around 30 minutes. In the past the crossing took much longer and could be hazardous. Before the introduction of a steamer service the passage was made by vessels under sail or with oars and crossing the main tidal stream could make the journey rough. Matters improved in 1830 when three Lymington businessmen bought a 51-ton wooden-hulled paddle steamer called *Glasgow*, then working on the Tyne. Six years later towboats were added for carrying across livestock and horses and carriages.

With the opening of the Brockenhurst to Lymington railway in 1858, the Solent Sea Co. added a second steamer, the *Red Lion*, to its

A 19th century engraving of the steam packet arriving at Ryde Pier towing a barge containing a carriage and horses.

The first purpose-built car ferry, MV Lymington, *berthed at Yarmouth, probably in the 1950s.*

BELOW *The paddle steamer* Gracie Fields *was bombed and sunk at Dunkirk in 1940.*

strength. In 1884 the London and South Western Railway took over the route and nine years later introduced a much larger paddle steamer to the service. A watershed came in 1938 with the arrival of *MV Lymington*, which was purpose-built to carry vehicles as well as foot passengers and brought an end to the life of the old tow boats. Since the withdrawal of *Freshwater* in 1959 all services have been vehicle carrying, and today three modern ferries operate the service.

In the 18th century many visitors to the Island preferred to stay overnight in the newly fashionable resort of Southampton, completing their journey the next morning on the sailing packet boat to Cowes. On a June night in 1799 a French privateer cut the Cowes packet from its moorings in Southampton, although it did not get far before running aground and being captured by sailors from Ryde. Nevertheless, the incident prompted the Admiralty to post a warship at each end of the Solent.

In 1820 George Ward of Cowes began a steam packet service on the Southampton-Cowes route and a rival service arrived on the scene six years later. In 1862 the wonderfully-named Southampton, Isle of Wight & South of England Royal Mail Steam Packet Co. Ltd began to operate the route and, as the much shorter Red Funnel Company, it remains in service today. Its first steamer was the wooden-hulled *Vectis*, built by Joseph White of Cowes and launched in 1866. The last paddle steamer was the *Gracie Fields* built at Southampton in 1936 and launched by its celebrated namesake (in a wartime broadcast the writer J.B. Priestley described it as

'the glittering queen of our local line). The *Gracie Fields* was requisitioned at the outbreak of the Second World War, ending its days off the Dunkirk beaches after being hit by a German bomb.

Another wartime casualty was the Southern Railway paddle steamer *Portsdown*, which struck a mine in 1940 on the mail run to Ryde from Portsmouth, with the loss of 20 lives.

The *Medina* was the first motor passenger ferry to work the Solent ferry service, starting in 1931 and remaining in service until 1962. As car ownership became more popular, new car ferries had to be built or existing ferries altered to accommodate them. In 1959 the *Carisbrooke Castle* was built to an entirely new design, enabling her to carry 45 cars. The first 'double ended' ferry, the *Netley Castle* came into service in 1974, carrying 80 cars.

The ferry service with the longest recorded history is the one between Portsmouth and Ryde. In 1420 the Abbey of Wherwell, which owned the shore and land in the Ryde area, claimed control of the boats used on the passage to and from Portsmouth. In the

next century the manorial court drew up regulations and fares, with a sailing vessel working the passage every day. By the late 18th century there was still only one sailing per day in each direction. At low tide passengers were landed on the beach and then brought to the upper part of the beach by horse and cart.

A significant improvement came in 1814 when the initial stage of Ryde Pier (at 2,250 feet now the fourth longest pier in England) was constructed, allowing passengers to disembark at all states of the tide. In 1862-64 a tramway pier was erected next to the original pier for the benefit of travellers. This was followed in 1880 by a railway pier which provided direct links with the rail network, encouraging more passengers to use the ferries, and the route became known as the 'Gateway to the Island'. The ferry crossing was operated by paddle steamers until 1948 when they were replaced by motor vessels which stayed in service until 1986. Today catamarans serve the route, completing the crossing in 15 minutes.

A fourth route to the Island opened in 1926 between Portsmouth and Fishbourne to serve the ever-growing trade in vehicle transportation. As the size of lorries increased, so the ferries have had to correspondingly grow in size. As many summer visitors now travel by car this route is very popular,

ABOVE *The hovercraft crossing from Ryde to Southsea takes 10 minutes.*

BELOW *The high speed 'Red Jet 3' arriving at Cowes from Southampton.*

with five large ferries providing a service every half hour throughout the summer.

The fastest route across the Solent is by hovercraft from Southsea to Ryde. This route opened in 1965 and takes 10 minutes. There is a connecting bus service between Southsea and the railway station at Portsmouth, making the route popular with regular commuters.

As the ferry services grow quicker and more frequent the Island seemingly gets nearer to the mainland. There is always talk of building a bridge or a tunnel to link the Island. Such matters have always been pipedreams in the minds of the instigators, and hopefully they will remain as such!

BRIGHSTONE (E)

Brighstone is the largest village in the Back of the Wight. More recent development has resulted in the expansion of the village and there is now a large residential area to the south of the historic centre. Brighstone is well placed for visiting the surrounding area, with attractive walks to the north up Rowdown Lane to the Downs, or south along Chilton Lane, past Chilton Farm and on to the coast.

The village centre is complete – with a church, school, post office, shops and pub. A stroll up North Street is rewarding. Here is the post office, the National Trust Shop and the Village Museum, all housed in attractive cottages. The Museum has an interesting exhibition showing village life in the 19th century, when farm workers' wages were about 10 shillings (50 pence) per week.

The Church of St Mary The Virgin is one of five churches on the Island with this dedication. The earliest part of the

Brighstone. North Street; one of the most attractive village streets in the Island (see also the colour section).

Brighstone. Thatched cottages; typical of the village.

building dates from the 12th century, but there are many later additions and alterations. Brighstone is unusual in having had three rectors who later became bishops. Thomas Ken (rector 1666-1668) became Bishop of Bath and Wells and wrote such hymns as 'Awake my Soul', Samuel Wilberforce (1830-1840) became Bishop of Oxford and George Moberly (1866-1869) became Bishop of Salisbury. The local inn is named The Three Bishops in their memory. The church has a fine 13th century chancel with four lancet windows. The arches in the panels of the Jacobean pulpit are designed to give the impression of perspective. The two oak sanctuary chairs were given in 1894 by the Victorian novelist and storyteller

for children, Charlotte Yonge, a friend of the then rector, Rev. W. Heygate.

Sites worth visiting in the area, and in easy walking distance, include Waytes Court, to the east end of the village, a picturesque stone farmhouse with stone mullioned windows and a thatched roof. The manorial court would have been held in the large room. In 1633 the manor was purchased for £2,500 by the historian Sir John Oglander, but he did not live here.

Brighstone water mill is mentioned in the Domesday Survey, but milling

Brighstone, Moortown Road. A curious carving of a sailing ship cut in chalk.

ceased in the last century and today the buildings have been developed into five dwellings. Marshgreen Farm House, with its stone mullioned window was built in 1606: it is now divided into two but the blocked in centre door can still be seen. Several of the older cottages and farm buildings in the area are constructed of the local chalk or dark brown ironstone. Some buildings opposite the junction with Moortown Road have curious carvings of sailing ships cut into the soft chalk. These probably date from the 18th or 19th centuries but their exact origin or purpose is unknown.

About a mile to the east of Brighstone is the hamlet of Limerstone. The site is said to be older than Brighstone, but all that can be seen today from the road is the rear of the manor house, which is a long low building with stone mullioned windows. On the other side of the road, which originally went through the yard, are some well-built stone farm buildings. Muggleton Lane has a few cottages.

The R.N.L.I. placed the first lifeboat on the Island at Brighstone in 1860 following the loss of 14 lives in a shipwreck the previous year. Much of the money was raised locally, and by the time the station closed in 1915 the lifeboat had been launched 46 times and saved 433 lives.

BROOK (E)

A one street village running from the foot of the Downs in the north to the Military Road and the coast in the south. On entering from the north a fine stone wall appears on the right. At one time it enclosed the grounds of the manor house, now hidden by trees. In about 1856 Charles Seely, a Nottinghamshire coal mine owner who had originally come to the Island as a boy to recover from a chest infection, purchased the Brook Estate and started to improve the house. He also bought most of the village, where in due course he built sturdy vernacular-style cottages for his workers. It was at Brook House in 1864 that he entertained Garibaldi, the Italian patriot, who planted an oak tree (now blown down) in front of the house. The village green with the stream on one side and a row of stone-built cottages on the other make for an attractive scene.

Brook. Brook House before it was reroofed and converted into flats in the 1950s.

On the Down behind the village is Brook Hill House, a large stone house built for Charles Seely's son, also called Charles (born 1833) and later the first baronet, to the designs of the architect Sir Aston Webb (he also designed Admiralty Arch and the Victoria & Albert Museum). The house was completed in 1915, the year in which Sir Charles died. During the 1950s it was occupied by the author and playwright J.B. Priestley: it has since been converted into flats.

Below the house is the Church of St Mary the Virgin. The present church was built in 1864 on the site of the medieval church, which had been destroyed by fire. Some of the fabric was salvaged and re-used, including the medieval door and windows. The local lifeboat was an important part of village

Brook Green. Ruins of the old Lifeboat Station.

ABOVE *Brook. Brook Hill House, completed in 1915 for Sir Charles Seely.*

RIGHT *Brook. The green and village hall (with bay wndows).*

life and on the west wall of the church is a board listing all the vessels attended by the lifeboat from 1866 until closure in 1937, during which time it saved 263 lives.

To the south of the village, beside the Military Road is a cluster of cottages called Brook Green. It was here that a Lifeboat Station was opened in 1860 (shortly after Brighstone). The boat had to be drawn from its house and down to the beach by a team of horses collected from nearby farms. The Seely family took a great interest in the Lifeboat Station, and Charles Seely's grandson John (1868-1947), known as Jack, became a crew member and during the 1930s served as a coxswain. In 1933, and by now a much decorated General following service in both the Boer and First World Wars, Jack Seely became the 1st Lord Mottistone (*also see* Mottistone).

The coastal path passes through

Brook Green and a bracing walk along to Compton Bay is rewarded with stunning views of the coast towards Freshwater Bay. About a mile along the shore towards Freshwater is Hanover Point where, at low tide, it is possible to see the remains of a petrified forest.

In the mid 19th century it was thought that the French might invade the Island. A War Department survey revealed that the south-west coast from Freshwater Bay to Chale was completely undefended. It was decided

to construct a military road along the coast so that troops and equipment could be quickly moved to repulse any invasion. The road gradually fell into disrepair and the War Department rented it to the adjoining landowners without any obligation to repair it. In 1930 it was bought by the County Council, who by using the unemployed were able to rebuild it. Today the Military Road provides a wonderful drive with lovely views in all directions.

Calbourne. Stone and old brick in the village centre.

CALBOURNE (E)

An attractive village with some fine buildings, it is perhaps best approached from the east where, about a mile outside the village, lies Swainston Manor House.

Now an hotel, the manor house is Georgian in style and was badly damaged by incendiary bombs in the Second World War. To the right of the front of the main building are some of the oldest domestic buildings on the Island, dating from the 12th and 13th centuries. One of them was an open hall house and has been partitioned off as a chapel. From before the Norman Conquest until 1285 the manor was held by Winchester Cathedral. Following a visit by Edward I, and a later dispute between king and the then bishop, it was seized by the crown. The manor passed through many hands and in the late 16th century it came to the Barrington family. In 1832 it was inherited by Louisa Edith Barrington, who married Sir Richard Simeon and it stayed in the family until the 1950s. A later Simeon, Sir John was a close friend of the Poet Laureate, Alfred Lord Tennyson, who often visited Swainston.

The centre of Calbourne, which has some well-built stone cottages, is to the south of a crossroads. One of the cottages on the right-hand side, marked with a plaque, was once the home of W.H. Long, 19th century author of *A Dictionary of the Isle of Wight Dialect*. A little further is the covered well and village pump, beyond which stands the parish Church of All Saints, one of five island churches mentioned in the Domesday Book.

The church is mainly 13th and early 19th century, with the more recent work produced in a faithful copy of the Early English style. The north transept contains the Barrington-Simeon Chapel, so named after the owners of Swainston Manor. In the chancel is a 17th century brass of Arthur Price, a Cromwellian rector, and in the south aisle there is a 14th century brass. Next to the church is the old rectory, stone-built and dating from the early 19th century.

More architectural highlights can be found at the end of the village. First, there is North East Lodge, a partly octagonal cottage in knapped flint. Round the corner is Calbourne's best known landmark, the line of 18th and 19th century cottages known as Winkle Street or Barrington Row. Facing the infant Caul Bourne, which flows north into Newton Creek, these picturesque stone and thatched cottages have long

BELOW *Calbourne Water Mill and Museum is a working water mill open to the public.*

BOTTOM *Calbourne. Westover House, designed by John Nash.*

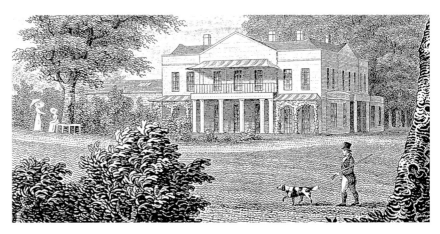

Carisbrooke. Cottages in the High Street with the parish church in the background.

Carisbrooke, the Church of St Mary. The memorial to Captain William Keeling.

been hugely popular (*see colour section*).

Behind the lodge and across the lake is Westover, a large classical-style house reconstructed in 1813-15 by John Nash. It was once the home of Colonel Moulton-Barrett, a relative of the poet, Elizabeth Barrett Browning. There are several interesting walks through the former Westover estate.

To the west of the village, on the road to Freshwater, is Calbourne Water Mill and Museum. By the entrance is a large gun barrel recovered from the beach – having been dumped there by Cliff End Battery, near Colwell Bay, when of no further use. The mill is open to the public during the summer and is the only working water mill on the Island. There are several attractions including a First and Second World War Museum, punting on the stream and a putting green, all set in 11 acres of landscaped valley.

CARISBROOKE (E)

Lying at the foot of the hilltop castle (*see* Defence of the Island), the village of Carisbrooke has, during the past century, become a suburb of Newport. The High Street, with its attractive range of stone and brick cottages, old

and new, winds up the hill with the castle on the left and the limestone Church of St Mary the Virgin on a ledge on the right.

This early Norman church was once part of a Benedictine Priory, built along the north wall, and was suppressed by Henry V in 1415. Stone from the priory was said to have been used to build the fine tower. The chancel was demolished in the 16th century, but the scar it left can still be seen on the outside of the church at the east end. The inside is well worth seeing, containing some fine tombs, including the canopied stone tomb of Lady Margaret Wadham under the north windows, and the sepulchral

slab in the centre aisle of the nave with a brass bearing the Keeling arms. Captain William Keeling discovered the coral Cocos (Keeling) Islands in the Indian Ocean in 1609. He became Captain of Cowes Castle, dying in 1619, aged 42. Also to be seen is the Puritan pulpit of 1658, with its back and tester.

Carisbrooke, the Church of St Mary.

Chale. The ancient church of St Andrew is at the south end of the parish, close to the coast.

Opposite the church is Castle Street, which leads down to a ford that can be crossed on foot and is an attractive way of approaching the castle. At the bottom of the High Street is the old waterworks and beside it, behind the houses, an open area with a large pond, grass banks and seats. Ideal for a picnic or simply feeding the ducks.

In the garden of the former vicarage a Roman villa was discovered and partly excavated in 1859. Today it is covered over and is not accessible to the public.

To the south of the village, on the Whitcombe Road, is the former St Dominic's Priory, Victorian Gothic of 1865-66, and now a Christian Retreat Centre.

There are several good walks around Carisbrooke, including one along Miller's Lane, at the foot of the castle, out into the Bowcombe Valley. Another walk offering excellent views is from Nodeham Lane into Down Lane and on across Bowcombe Down.

CHALE (1)

A small village situated between Chale Down and the exposed coast of Chale Bay in the Back of the Wight. The stretch of coast between Blackgang Chine and Brighstone is the most desolate and windswept on the Island, infamous for shipwrecks and smuggling. Chale sensibly stands well back from the sea, and the heart of the village is tucked under St Catherine's Down around the junction of Church Place, the Military Road and Blythe Shute. Here lies St Andrew's Church.

Although most of the present building is 15th century, the original dates from three centuries earlier. The churchyard has many fascinating if weather-beaten tombstones, some of which mark the graves of those who lost their lives in shipwrecks, including 18 from the *Clarendon*, a squarerigger wrecked in Chale Bay in 1836: one buried elsewhere is a Miss Gourlay, whose corpse finally washed up in front of her father's house in Southsea. Inside, the church is dark (there is a light switch for those wishing to read the memorials), although this only serves to increase the

visual impact of the splendid 19th century stained glass windows.

Almost opposite the church is the village primary school, part of which is still housed in its original 1843 building. At the north end of Church Place, on the right, is a fine 17th century stone house, which is well worth seeking out.

Close by is Chale Abbey Farm. Parts of the 14th century hall house, together with a fine Gothic window still exist. It was built for John de Langford, Warden of Carisbrooke Castle. The house is not open to the public.

Opposite the house is a car park, a useful landmark for those wishing to take advantage of the area's many excellent walks. Upper House Lane, at the northern end of Church Place, becomes a footpath, which leads to St Catherine's Down. Visible at the north end of the Down is the Hoy Monument, a tall stone column. It was erected in 1814 by Michael Hoy, a merchant trading with Russia, to commemorate the visit of Tsar Alexander I: ironically, a later tablet at the foot of the column honours those who died fighting the Russians at Inkerman and Sebastapol in the Crimean War.

Chale. The Hoy Monument on St Catherine's Down.

of Urry, who also had land at Afton, near Freshwater, and at Thorley. The massive oak beams, given by Sir William Oglander in 1605 to Thomas Urry on his marriage to Jane Day, still can be seen in the attic – four centuries later. Beside it is a ford which leads to a footpath through the woods to Gatcombe Church, where there is a memorial to Thomas and Jane's eldest son, another Thomas (died 1671).

Farther along the main road is the school, which serves the village and much of the surrounding area, and has a well-designed recent extension. Opposite the school is the former Bible Foundation Chapel, built in 1860. By

LEFT *Chessell. Shalcombe Manor House.*

BELOW *Chillerton. The main street with the village school on the right.*

BOTTOM *Chillerton. Sheat Manor House built in the early 17th century for the ancient Island family of Urry.*

About 1½ miles north of Chale on the Newport road is Chale Green. This hamlet has an attractive green with houses on both sides. This is an ideal place from which to start a walk, and there are numerous to choose from.

CHESSELL (E)

There are two good reasons for stopping in the hamlet of Chessell, which lies south of the Newport-Freshwater Road. One is Shalcombe Manor, which has a date stone of 1683 and is thought to have once been a mill with a house in an adjoining field. The second is Chessell Pottery, well-known for its decorative porcelain. The pottery (plus café and shop) is open to the public throughout the year, and visitors can watch the potters at work or try their hand themselves.

The nearby downs provide excellent walks and superb views.

CHILLERTON (F)

The village is situated in a downland hollow and stretches along part of the Newport to Chale road. Chillerton is overshadowed by the Down with its ancient barrows and a tall communications mast. It is mainly made up of modern houses.

From the north the first building of interest is the Jacobean Sheat Manor House, built in the E-plan style with gabled wings and a porch. The house was built for the ancient Island family

Colwell. The Bay with the 19th century Fort Albert on the water's edge.

COWES (B)

It is said that the best way to approach Cowes is by sea, but those who wish to understand the town's history would do better to enter Cowes across the River Medina by the chain ferry from East Cowes. The crossing provides views both up and down the river, reveals much of what has made Cowes famous, and gives a good flavour of its atmosphere and character.

The best way to see the relationship between Cowes and East Cowes is from the air, as in the aerial photograph in the colour section.

Prior to the 18th century Cowes was just a collection of a few houses. Sir John Oglander, the 17th century historian, wrote, 'I have known when there were not above three or four houses in Cowes'. In the second half of the century the town started to grow, the houses clustered round the castle of 1539 and those further inland merging to form the 'new white builte Maritime town of Cowes'. The 18th century left a legacy of bow-fronted town houses, some with oriel windows or balconies; but by the early part of the 19th century it was in a sorry state, with poor housing, narrow potholed roads and all the problems associated with a lack of sanitation and hygiene. By then it was the main port for the Island, trading

the stream can be seen the old village sheepwash.

The centre of the village is the Green, which was re-landscaped to mark the millennium. On the edge of the open area is the old Methodist chapel. After an extensive restoration in 1982 the stone-built building is now a community centre. Opposite is the working men's club, housed in a building which was once the village school.

There are several good walks in the area; one of which is up Hollow Lane and over the hill to Ramsdown Farm.

About two miles south of Chillerton is Billingham, which consists of a farm, a few cottages and, on the left, a mainly 18th century stone and brick built manor house. From 1933 to 1947 this was the home of J.B. Priestley O.M. (1894-1984), the author and playwright (*The Good Companions, An Inspector Calls* etc) (*see also* 'Writers and Poets').

COLWELL (D)

The Ward Lock *Guide* of 1907-08 had this to say about Colwell: '. . . good bathing is to be had, and those who like an unsophisticated and out-of-the-world place might do worse than give it a trial.' In many respects those words hold true today, although the village has

grown to become, essentially, a part of Freshwater. Most of the housing is recently built, some as holiday accommodation. To the north of the main road to Freshwater is the attractive common, on the edge of which is an early Baptist church. Built in 1836, it is still in use as a place of worship today.

From the common a road leads down to Colwell Bay and Esplanade, where there are fine views over to Hurst Castle and the mainland. There are a couple of popular walks from the Esplanade: one north towards Cliff End and another south along the coastal path to Totland Bay.

Cowes. Sun Hill; a good idea of what the town was like in the early 19th century.

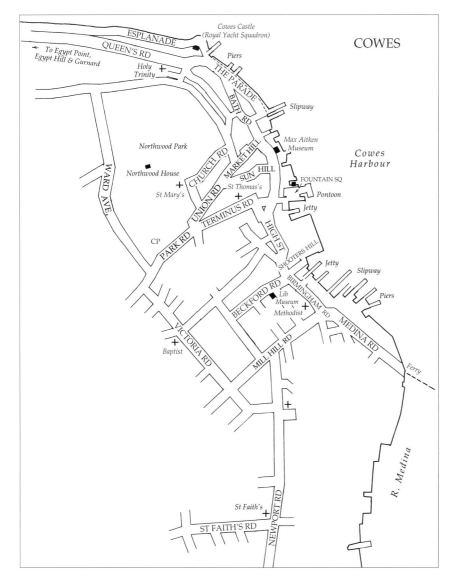

COWES

Cowes Castle (Royal Yacht Squadron)

To Egypt Point, Egypt Hill & Gurnard

ESPLANADE
QUEEN'S RD
Piers
Holy Trinity
THE PARADE
BATH RD
Slipway
Cowes Harbour
Northwood Park
Max Aitken Museum
CHURCH RD
MARKET HILL
Northwood House
SUN HILL
FOUNTAIN SQ
UNION RD
St Thomas's
Pontoon
St Mary's
TERMINUS RD
Jetty
WARD AVE.
PARK RD
CP
HIGH ST
SHOOTERS HILL
Jetty
Slipway
BECKFORD RD
BIRMINGHAM RD
Lib Museum
Piers
Methodist
MEDINA RD
VICTORIA RD
Baptist
MILL HILL RD
Ferry
R. Medina
St Faith's
NEWPORT RD
ST FAITH'S RD

extensively with North America. Cargoes were often unloaded here, repacked and then forwarded to the Netherlands or Germany. This increase in trade naturally spawned an expansion in shipbuilding and repair yards.

Another factor in the town's expansion was the growing popularity of yachting among royalty and the aristocracy. Large houses and villas sprung up for the wealthy when they arrived for the yachting season.

The central car park is at the junction of Ward Avenue and Park Road. Close by in Church Road is St Mary's Church which dates from 1867, but the first place of worship on this site was a Puritan chapel of 1657. The tower, saved from an earlier building, was designed by John Nash.

It is possible to gauge what old West Cowes was like by walking along the nearby Union Road and down Market Hill to the High Street. The turning to the right passes the Sir Max Aitken Museum, which contains a collection of the famous yachtsman's nautical instruments and paintings. It is housed in an old sail loft and is open during the summer. Further along the High Street is the Fountain Hotel, built in 1804, with its archway leading to Fountain Pier, terminal of the 'Red Jet' – a fast ferry service to and from Southampton.

Cowes. A fine example of weatherboarding and gable windows.

Cowes. The Maritime Museum. The model in the glass case is of the paddle steamer Waverley, *which visits the Island each year.*

LEFT *Cowes. The Parade in the mid 1920s.*

BELOW LEFT *Cowes. Princes Green during Cowes Week.*

Cowes, and there is a plaque on the house, which was originally named Birmingham Hall and built in 1752 for Lord Mount Edgcumbe.

Turning left into Medina Road, there on the right is Ratsey & Lapthorn. The firm of Ratseys, sailmakers, have been in business for over 200 years. Further along on the right is a red brick building which was the offices of the famous shipbuilders, John Samuel White (*see* East Cowes). The road ends with the slipway down to the chain ferry to East Cowes.

Retrace your steps back along the High Street to its junction with Market Hill. Nearby are the Macnamara Almshouses, a terrace of six houses for the sick and aged of Cowes founded by the rector of Kingston in 1881. From Market Hill walk on into Bath Road which leads on to the Parade. Here is a popular place to park and enjoy the views out over the Harbour towards Southampton Water. The Parade is dominated by Osborne Court, a tall block of flats built in the Art-Deco style in 1935-36. Nearby, a brass plaque recalls the *Dove* and the *Ark*, who anchored at Cowes in 1633 when westbound across the Atlantic with 200 settlers on board to found the State of Maryland. At the north end of the Parade is Cowes Castle, the oldest building in the area. It was built on the orders of Henry VIII in 1539 and along with another castle – long since disappeared – on the East Cowes side, guarded the Harbour entrance. The semicircular platform, where once 12 cannon faced out to sea, is the oldest surviving part.

Today the Castle is famous as the home of the Royal Yacht Squadron, whose bronze cannon, taken from William IV's yacht *Royal Adelaide*, traditionally fire the start of the races during Cowes Week in early August. Sailing and Cowes are today

Next door to the hotel is the Vectis Tavern: 16th century and part timber framed. Continuing along the street, Shooters Hill is reached and from there into Birmingham Road.

In Beckford Road (a turning off Birmingham Road) is Cowes Library, which is also home to Cowes Maritime Museum. This tells the town's story, and houses a display of model boats relating to the town's maritime past.

On the right hand side of Birmingham Road is the world famous marine photographers Beken of Cowes. Frank Beken first took pictures of the yachts racing in the Solent in around 1890, a tradition continued by his son Keith and grandson Kenneth.

A little further along is the Methodist Church. Almost opposite is the red brick house where Dr. Thomas Arnold – the famous Victorian headmaster of Rugby School was born in 1795. His father was the collector of customs at synonymous. Cutter racing round the Island goes back to the late 18th century. In 1815, the year of Waterloo, a group of gentlemen with a common interest in yachting formed what was initially called The Yacht Club (the Royal was added when George IV joined). Annual regattas at Cowes gave way in 1826 to organized racing. When 'Sailor Billy', William IV, became king the Club was renamed the Royal Yacht Squadron, acquiring West Cowes Castle as its headquarters in 1854 and converting it into a club house. Under the patronage of the Prince of Wales (later Edward VII) the prestige of the Squadron grew – and with it Cowes.

Today yacht racing is more democratic than during its Edwardian heyday. For one week in high summer the town is transformed into an international festival of sail and thronged with visitors. Yachts crowd the pontoons. Every pub is packed with men and women in oilskins. Flags fly from the club houses lining the Parade. Finally, a spectacular firework display held on the Friday evening brings the curtain down on Cowes Week, and

Cowes. In the centre is Holy Trinity Church, and on the right is Cowes Castle, now the headquarters of the Royal Yacht Squadron.

Racing during Cowes Week.

Cowes reverts to its staider quieter self.

On rising ground behind the Royal Yacht Squadron is Holy Trinity Church, the oldest C. of E. church in Cowes. Built in 1832 of distinctive yellow brick, it is known as the 'Yachtsmen's Church'. Inside are memorials to past members of the Squadron: outside in the gardens is the stone Fastnet Memorial, erected in memory of the 15 yachtmen who died in the 1979 Fastnet

Race. To the west of the castle is the Esplanade and Princes Green. Here are some of the fine marine villas built by the wealthy as Cowes grew fashionable: the Earl of Belmore's 'Belmore', Beaulieu House, where the exiled Emperor Napoleon III and the Empress Eugénie once spent an autumn – and 'Rosetta', in whose garden in 1873 Winston Churchill's father successfully proposed to a young American, Jennie

Cowes. On the high ground above the town is Northwood House, built in the early 19th century for the wealthy Ward family.

Jerome, whose own ancestors had left the Island early in the 18th century. Today it is a National Trust holiday cottage.

A popular walk is along the Esplanade towards Egypt Point and on to Gurnard. It was on the shore adjoining Cowes Castle that sea bathing was first recorded in 1760. Soon small huts on wheels called bathing machines carried the bather across the beach and into the shallows. At Egypt Point is the now disused Egypt Light of 1897, which became redundant when the adjacent buoys were rearranged.

On the east side of Ward Avenue is the Italianate Northwood House, the former home of the Ward family, who owned much of the land on which the town was built. William Ward (1787-1849) is today remembered as a famous cricketer who bought the lease of Lord's Cricket Ground in London to save it from being sold for building purposes in 1825. Today, the grounds of the house are open to the public and are worth a visit.

In Terminus Road is the Roman Catholic Church of St Thomas of Canterbury, built in 1796, five years after its counterpart in Newport, making it the second oldest Catholic church on the Island. In Victoria Road is the Baptist Chapel of 1877; whilst on the outskirts of the town, in Newport Road, is the Church of St Faith of 1909. Nearby is Northwood Cemetery, which lovers of trees find worth visiting.

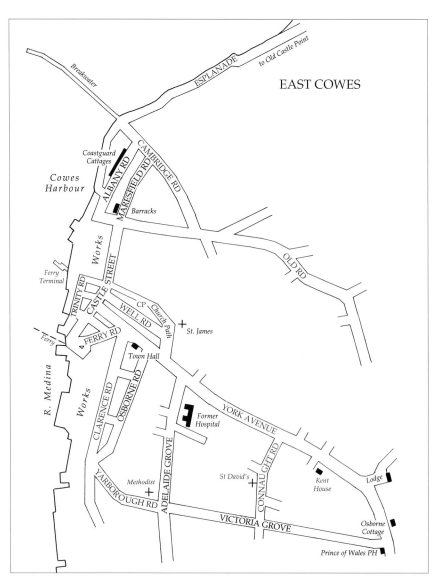

CRANMORE (E)

No other residential area on the Island has the same atmosphere as Cranmore. Before the 19th century most of it was brickyards or open fields belonging to Cranmore Farm, but in 1898 William Carter formed a company called Homesteads Ltd and bought 375 acres for development. The land was divided into 168 smallholdings and house plots and several roads were also laid, linked at The Green. For some years there was little enthusiasm for the project: eventually it was hoped that soldiers returning from the First World War would farm the smallholdings. However, the soil was poor and many potential buyers opted for emigration

and the Canadian government's offer of 160 acres of land free. By the outbreak of the Second World War there had been some take-up and around 90 houses were built.

This unusual story and the piecemeal development have made for an interesting range of architectural styles, ranging from the original Homestead bungalows to modern homes. In 1963 part of Cranmore was designated an Area of Outstanding Natural Beauty to save the area from being built on and to conserve the wildlife and its habitats. The Green was cleared and seats provided. There are several walks, including one to the north along the coastal path.

EAST COWES (B)

The casual visitor to the East Cowes of today would need a considerable feat of imagination to envisage the rich history of the town. In the 17th century it was certainly more important than Cowes, which was then little more than a collection of cottages. East Cowes owes its growth to its importance as a centre for shipbuilding, indeed one of the local shipwrights, Joseph Nye, travelled to Russia to assist Peter the Great in the establishment of the Russian Navy.

Shipbuilding in East Cowes – principally for the Royal Navy – dates chiefly from the mid 18th century. The wars with France meant there was a demand for ships. Builders such as Joseph Nye, Thomas White, Phileman Ewer and Daniel List flourished as a succession of ships rolled from their yards into the Medina. The end of the Napoleonic Wars and the gradual change from timber to iron lead to closure or amalgamation. By the mid 20th century there was one yard building warships, two building lifeboats for the R.N.L.I., and a number of small yards constructing pleasure craft.

The warships were built by the well-known firm of John Samuel White, which originally came to East Cowes in about 1803 when Thomas White transferred his yard from Kent. Within 50 years White's had built 40,000 tons of merchant shipping and had slipways on the East Cowes river bank and fitting-out berths on the Cowes side. As sail surrendered to steam, their designers turned their attention to torpedo boats and destroyers for the Royal Navy, as well as lifeboats, paddleboats and ferries. After the Second World War costs rose and

The view from East Cowes across the river to Cowes showing the hammerhead crane built for J.S. White in 1911.

East Cowes. An aerial photograph of 1934 showing the shipbuilding slipways of J.S. White. Across the River Medina in Cowes are the fitting out quays and hammerhead crane. To the right, a chain ferry is about to cross the river. The two ships under construction in the slipways at East Cowes were the destroyers Forester *and* Fury.

demand fell, leading to the closure of the yard in 1981. But one White's built destroyer, H.M.S. *Cavalier*, launched in 1944, has been preserved and is now berthed at Chatham Historic Dockyard. Its propeller, however, can be seen on the nearby Esplanade. White's large hammerhead crane of 1911 still stands on the Cowes side of the River Medina as a permanent reminder of their

contribution to the history of both towns.

Another large employer was Saunders-Roe, who first opened for business in East Cowes in 1906. They mainly built aeroplanes and motor launches. During the Second World War the firm grew rapidly and began to produce Walrus and Sea Otter aircraft. After the war Saunders-Roe built the huge SR45 Princess flying boats, but the airlines lost interest in flying boats and production was stopped. Later Saunders-Roe built the prototype of the first hovercraft, and in due course their Columbine Works became the home of the British Hovercraft Corporation. The firm, now called GKN, has moved up river and the large shed, instantly recognisable by the huge Union flag painted on its doors, has passed to new owners.

In the late 18th and early 19th

centuries, the combination of yachting and coastal scenery attracted the wealthy and fashionable to East Cowes. In 1798 John Nash (1752-1835), the celebrated architect, had East Cowes Castle built as his residence (allowed to become derelict, it was demolished in 1962, and the site is now occupied by modern housing). Nash, whose principal works include the Royal Pavilion in Brighton and Buckingham Palace, also left a considerable architectural legacy on the Island. His buildings include churches in Bembridge, Cowes, East Cowes and Whippingham; the Guildhall and Isle of Wight County Club in Newport; as well as lodges and alterations to country houses.

At about the same time, Lord Henry Seymour had Norris Castle erected on high ground to the north-east of the town. This pseudo-medieval castle,

designed by James Wyatt, is still standing and is best seen from the sea. Visitors to East Cowes in this period included the Prince Regent (later George IV) and the artist J.M.W. Turner, who came twice, the second time in 1827 when commissioned by Nash to paint a series of paintings of the castle and shipping.

One of the most attractive ways of approaching the heart of the town is to travel the full length of York Avenue. This road, plus Victoria Grove and Adelaide Grove, formed the edge of a fashionable mid 19th century housing scheme for the gentry. The land had been purchased by George Brooks, a London land agent, who optimistically presumed that the proximity of Queen

East Cowes. Norris Castle was erected for Lord Henry Seymour in 1798.

Victoria's home at Osborne, a harbour, several leading yacht clubs and a mild climate, would attract wealthy families to have villas built. Named East Cowes Park Estate, the plots were arranged around a central botanic garden of 22 acres. Only about a quarter of the plots sold, and Brooks fled to France to escape his creditors. Today the garden has been built over and only a handful of the houses are still standing, including Kent House, once the home of Earl Mountbatten's parents (who are buried in Whippingham churchyard), and Osborne Cottage which was, for a period, the residence of Princess Beatrice (1857-1944), the much-loved youngest daughter of Queen Victoria, who was for many years Governor of the Island.

Near the 'Prince of Wales' public house in York Avenue are a pair of cottage villas with solid concrete walls. Built in 1852, they are early examples of the use of shuttered concrete in domestic buildings.

At the western end of York Avenue is the former Town Hall, built in 1896 at the time of the establishment of an Urban District Council. Nearby is the Church of St James, erected to a Nash design in 1831. Appropriately, the architect is buried at the foot of the tower. The foundation stone was laid by Princess Victoria, the future Queen, although the church was substantially rebuilt in 1868 with only the tower surviving.

In Connaught Road is the Roman Catholic Church of St David, built in 1957 to replace two earlier buildings, and on the corner of Adelaide Grove and Yarborough Road is the yellow and red brick Methodist Chapel of 1897. To the rear is the old chapel, which was erected in 1859. There are two carved stone entrances to the classroom, one marked 'Scholars' and the other 'Teacher'.

East Cowes. The Town Hall of 1896.

Another building worth seeing in Adelaide Grove is the former Frank James Memorial Hospital, which owes its construction to an elephant. In 1890 the wealthy explorer Frank James was killed by an elephant whilst exploring in West Africa. His two brothers decided to build an almshouse for aged sailors in Frank's memory, choosing East Cowes because he was a member of the Royal Yacht Squadron. The attractive red brick building with its central block opened in 1893 to accommodate 12 seamen. There was soon an urgent need for hospital places for wounded soldiers returning from the Boer War, so its inmates were found other accommodation. After the end of the war the James brothers offered the almshouse to Princess Beatrice, the Island Governor, on condition that the building was used as a Cottage Hospital for the East Cowes area. It continued to be used as a hospital, and only closed recently in 2001.

East Cowes. The Frank James Memorial Hospital before it closed in 2001.

East Cowes Esplanade has good views over the entrance to the Harbour and is an excellent place to watch vessels of all shapes and sizes coming and going. The Red Funnel car ferry service runs between Southampton and East Cowes.

On joining the Esplanade from the town, the first building of interest is the brick-built Victoria Barracks, erected in 1872 to house Queen Victoria's guard. The army continued to occupy the building until 1960 when it became a factory. Next is a fine range of former coastguard cottages, together with the chief officer's house, which were built in 1891 to replace an older station in the town.

Close to the Esplanade, in Cambridge Road, is an attractive terrace of 1870s houses with distinctive wrought iron canopies and balconies.

There are several interesting walks in the area, including one along the entire length of the Esplanade to Old Castle Point. Another is to Whippingham Church and from there along the river to the Folly Inn.

FISHBOURNE (B)

Lying at the mouth of Wootton Creek, Fishbourne is now where visitors who have travelled by ferry from Portsmouth get their first close look at the Island. The route was introduced in 1927 to replace the barges towed by a tug that carried vehicles to and from the Island, and which were unloaded on a slipway at Ryde. Because the tide goes out a long way at Ryde, and loading and unloading could only take place at high tide, the schedule was changed daily. Fishbourne, at the mouth of Wootton Creek, was the nearest suitable place at which ferries could operate at all states of the tide.

Ferry terminals are not usually the most attractive of places and there is far more to this hamlet – which is situated on the main Ryde-Newport road – than merely the ferry. Beyond the terminal is the local pub and a small but extremely attractive green, surrounded by cottages. On the far side a road leads to an open space by the shore, an ideal spot for watching the creek's busy nautical life. The Royal Victoria Yacht Club is based at Fishbourne, and, in the early 19th century there was a shipyard which built yachts and coastal vessels.

There is a pleasant walk from Fishbourne through the lanes past Quarr Abbey and on to Ryde.

Fishbourne. The Portsmouth ferry arriving.

The 'Discovery' of the Isle of Wight

The early 19th century Royal Sandrock Hotel, Niton, was one of the first hotels to be built on the Island for visitors attracted by its climate and scenery. It was visited by Princess Victoria before she became Queen. Now destroyed.

The transformation of the Isle of Wight into the island we know today began in the 18th century and was inextricably linked to dramatic changes that were happening on the mainland. This seismic shift came as Great Britain changed rapidly from an agricultural economy to an industrial one. The catalyst for the transformation was a number of wars fought overseas that led to blockades of imports and created the need for increased production of food and other goods.

This, in turn, led to a dramatic improvement in transport and communications, firstly through the construction of canals, then with the expansion of the road network and finally, in the 19th century, with the coming of the railways. All these developments combined to encourage the 'arrival' of the Isle of Wight in the national consciousness.

Not that the Island's existence was a closely guarded secret before then. It had been of strategic importance, and was considered vulnerable to invasion by an enemy wanting it as a base from which to strike at the mainland. The French attacked several times and Spain was also thought to have a covetous eye on the Island during the 16th century. During the Civil War the Island was thrust into the spotlight when Charles I was imprisoned in Carisbrooke Castle.

However, it was in the 18th century that life on the Island really began to change. The catalyst was industrialisation, which created new wealth and led to the introduction of the concept of tourism, and the linked developments in transport. Improvements in the roads from London to the south coast enabled stage-coach travellers to reach Portsmouth and Southampton in the same day, although the gentry, with time to spare, still preferred more leisurely journeys.

Touring Britain in search of the 'picturesque' gradually became highly fashionable. The Lake District, the Scottish Highlands and southern England were especially popular. Isle of Wight shared in this boom. From the outset there was the enjoyable marriage of a pleasantly short sea journey accompanied by beautiful coastal views. Once safely ashore, the Island provided rugged cliffs, downland, woodland, unspoilt villages and hamlets. A popular attraction was the haunting ruins of Carisbrooke Castle, with their royal story to tell. Other visitors marvelled at the natural beauty and charm of the coast, in particular the chines.

As sea bathing became increasingly fashionable the broad sandy beaches with their lines of bathing machines provided privacy and an easy way into the sea. The first bathing machines were introduced at Cowes in 1771 and then at Ryde a few years later. The appreciation and enjoyment of these natural qualities were enhanced by the mild climate, which when combined with clean air, the bracing 'ozone', promoted good health.

By 1774 the gentry had begun to include the Island in their tours during 'the season' – August and September – possibly as a result of contact with the more fashionable resident families such as the Worsleys at Appledurcombe, the Blachfords at Osborne and the Barringtons at Swainston. In September 1776 an anonymous visitor crossed over from Lymington to Yarmouth, then travelled by post chaise to Newport, '. . . a neat and pretty town'. An excursion was made to Appledurcombe, the seat of Sir Robert Worsley, '. . . which is now rebuilding in a modern style with Portland stone the entrance and a large hall, with two rows of composite pillars.'

These early tourists were followed by others who, charmed by what the Island had to offer, began to build mansions and seaside villas. These included St Johns for Colonel Amherst, Fernhill for Thomas Orde (later Lord Bolton and Governor of the Isle of Wight) and The Priory for Sir Nash Grose. A William Brewster, visiting the Island in May 1791, recorded that he crossed over from Portsmouth to Ryde, later visiting the Priory at Nettlestone – 'one of the most beautiful places on the Island, nothing can exceed the beauty of the situation.' He also wrote of the magnificence of the cliffs at Freshwater, and the experience of reaching a cave at their foot.

Towards the end of the century leading architects were being brought to the Island to design grand residences, including James Wyatt, who designed Norris Castle for Lord Henry Seymour. John Nash, the famed Regency architect, built East Cowes Castle for his own use, entertaining Princess Victoria (later Queen Victoria) there.

The huge increase in the numbers of visitors led to an improvement in the accommodation on offer. In the second half of the 18th century several inns were enlarged, not only in the landing places of Cowes and Ryde, but also in the market town of Newport

and in the scenic Undercliff area. In the early years of the 19th century the first hotel was built, at Ryde, and by 1830 there were at least six hotels around the resorts.

In 1758 the landlord of the Bugle Inn, Newport, began offering a four-wheeled chaise for hire and within a few years the inns at Cowes, Ryde and Newport had one-horse chaises for hire, complete with a boy to act as guide and open the many gates. In 1770 the first stagecoach on the Island started its service between the Fountain Inn, Cowes, and the Sun Inn, Newport. It ran twice a day in each direction and met the packet boats upon their arrival at Cowes. By 1806 a coach service was also operating between Ryde and Newport.

The tourists who came to 'discover' the Isle of Wight were both assisted and encouraged in their travels by the early guidebooks. The artist John Hassell wrote of his journey to the Island in 1789 and it was published in two volumes in the following year. Upon leaving Cowes for the mainland he wrote: 'We have now finished our account of this pleasant, fertile, and happy spot; and from the observations we had an opportunity

A Victorian engraving showing the bathing machines to the right of Cowes Castle.

Shanklin Chine remains one of the original popular attractions still open to the public.

of making during our stay there, we were confirmed in the opinion which induced us to visit it, that for beautiful and picturesque views, select parts of it are scarcely exceeded by those on any other coasts.'

Four years later saw the publication of *A Picture of the Isle of Wight* by Henry Wyndham – the first true guide to the Island. Wyndham suggested inns at which to stay, transport that could be hired, and possible daily outings. He also gave his opinion of the various towns and villages. Of Cowes he wrote: '. . . the streets are narrow and ill built . . . The bathing, for the use of which there are four machines, is excellent; and the lodgings are numerous.' Ryde he thought 'a populous village, and the principal thoroughfare from the Island to Portsmouth. It has two tolerable inns, with chaises and whiskies; many decent lodgings are also to be hired in the place.'

The picturesque and romantic scenery of the Island attracted many artists as visitors in the late 18th and early 19th centuries, including George Morland, John Nixon and J.M.W. Turner. The resulting paintings in turn attracted more visitors to the Island, to see the views which had inspired the works of art. Not only that, the painters, in their various styles, produced an invaluable record of the Island in its early period as a holiday resort.

In 1820 the first steam ferries started to operate in the Solent, on the Southampton to Cowes route. This lead to a faster and more reliable service, which in turn attracted more visitors.

By the early 19th century several guide books were available, some written and printed by Islanders. Accommodation had also greatly improved and by 1840 there were at least 16 hotels open for business. Their rooms were soon filled, for that same year saw the opening of the London to Southampton railway. For the first time, the Island was within easy reach of the London middle classes. The *Hampshire Telegraph* of May 1840 noted that, 'Visitors have been flocking to the Island, and there is every appearance of a full and long season'. In the following year *The Times* stated that it was possible to make a day trip from London to the Island: the train to Southampton was followed by a trip around the Island on a steamer, returning to Southampton in time to catch a return train – stepping on to a London platform at 9.35 in the evening.

A few years later *The Times* was carrying advertisements tempting the would-be day tripper with excursions from London to Cowes, staying six hours on the Island, and returning to London in the evening. The Isle of Wight had established itself as a popular holiday and day trip destination.

FRESHWATER (D)

The village gets its name from the spring which rises about 200 yards from the beach at Freshwater Bay and flows north into the widening River Yar. It is the largest village in West Wight and grew during the 19th century to encompass the hamlets of Weston, Norton, Easton, Sutton and Middleton – although several of the names remain in use.

The Bay is small with a steeply shelving beach consisting mostly of pebbles. It is very popular, and has a car park close by. Until a few years ago there was an arched rock at the east end of the Bay, but today only its chalk stumps can be seen.

Across the road is Afton Marsh Nature Reserve, more than 25 acres of fen and grazing marsh on the Western Yar's old flood plain. Walks through the marshes offer a chance to see a variety of wildlife, including a wide range of birds and insects.

With its beach, downland walks and wonderful views out to sea, Freshwater Bay became a powerful magnet for eminent Victorian artists and intellectuals. Chief among these was Alfred Lord Tennyson (1809-1892), the celebrated poet, who fell in love with Farringford House when visiting the Island. With the proceeds from his poetry, in particular 'In Memoriam' and 'Maud', he decided to first rent the house in 1853 and then three years later

to purchase it for £6,900. The principal elevation with the main entrance is thought to be 18th century and the rest of the building dates from the 19th century. In 1867, driven to distraction by the numbers of tourists trying to get a glimpse of him, he had a house built on Blackdown Hill, West Sussex, called 'Aldworth' and escaped there, only returning to Farringford for the winter months. While in residence he received a string a well-known visitors, including fellow poets William Allingham and Henry Longfellow, Prince Albert, the author Lewis Carroll and Ellen Terry, the actress. After Tennyson's death in 1892 the family continued to live at Farringford until after the Second World War when it was sold and became an hotel. Among the works Tennyson published while at Farringford are 'The Charge of the Light Brigade' (1855), 'Maud' (1855), Idylls of the King' (1859), 'Enoch Arden' (1864) and 'The Foresters' (1892) (*see also* 'Writers and Poets').

Five years after his death a cross of

Freshwater Bay, showing its steeply shelving beach. On the headland is the remains of Freshwater Fort.

Cornish granite was erected on High Down, on the side of the old Freshwater beacon (*for illustration see* 'Enjoy the High Ground'). The inscription reads, 'In Memory of Alfred Lord Tennyson this cross is raised. A Beacon to Sailors, by the People of Freshwater and other Friends in England and America'. The monument was unveiled in 1897, and is now maintained by Trinity House as a seamark.

Another distinguished Victorian resident of Freshwater was Julia Margaret Cameron (1815-1879), the pioneering Victorian photographer. She lived at Dimbola Lodge, near the Bay, and the house is now open to the public with a permanent museum to her work and photographic exhibitions throughout the year (*see* 'Museums').

In Gate Lane is the Church of St Agnes, the only thatched church on the Island. Despite its ancient appearance, it was built as recently as 1908 using local stone. In contrast, All Saints Church in Church Place is one of the Island's oldest churches. Although it is recorded in the Domesday Book, the present building is early 13th century with the addition of a 15th century tower and further extensions in the 19th century. There is some fine Victorian stained glass. All Saints is where the Tennyson family worshipped and the grave of Emily Lady Tennyson can be found in the churchyard (her husband was buried in Westminster Abbey).

Hooke Road, the road from Church Place to School Green, recalls Robert Hooke (1635-1703), 'England's Leonardo' and one of the greatest of all natural scientists, to whom a memorial has recently been unveiled in Westminster Abbey. Hooke's father was rector of Freshwater, and to the son we owe the invention of the iris diaphragm in cameras, the universal joint in motor vehicles, the balance wheel in a watch, the word 'cell' in biology, and the first reflecting telescope.

In the north of the village is Golden Hill Fort, built from 1863 to cover the coastal forts, and including a barracks for more than 130 soldiers. During the

Freshwater. Farringford House, once the home of the poet Alfred Lord Tennyson.

Freshwater. The causeway crossing the Eastern Yar River. To the left, above the handrail, can be seen a Second World War pillbox.

First World War it was used as a training depot and in the Second World War British and Canadian troops were stationed there. Today it is private housing.

There are several good walks around the village, including the Freshwater Way, which starts at Freshwater Bay and travels north to Yarmouth. Another recommended route is over Afton Down through the golf course, and a third is from Freshwater Bay over Tennyson Down, past the Memorial Cross and on to Alum Bay.

Freshwater. The Church of St Agnes is the only thatched church on the Island.

GATCOMBE (F)

With no public transport and no through road, Gatcombe must be the quietest hamlet on the Isle of Wight. It lies south of Carisbrooke and is reached along a narrow lane off the Carisbrooke to Chillerton road.

On the left-hand side, before reaching the hamlet, is the Church of St Olave, which nestles at the foot of New Barn Down, and is entered through a porch of 1910 made from timbers from HMS *Thunderer*. The church is Perpendicular, apart from the mid 19th century chancel. There is some glorious 15th century stained glass near the pulpit, and the east window contains some fine examples of Pre-Raphaelite stained glass by the William Morris group, 1865-66. In the chancel is a 14th century carved oak effigy of a Crusading knight, and the nave contains a striking memorial to Charles Grant Seely, eldest son of the second Sir Charles Seely, who joined the Isle of Wight Rifles and was killed in action in Palestine in 1917 (*also see* Brook and Mottistone).

Gatcombe Park, a mid-18th century manor house, can be seen from the back of the churchyard, although it is best viewed from the road to Chillerton. It was built in 1750 on the site of an earlier house for Sir Edward Worsley, member of a branch of an influential Island family (*see* Wroxall). An ancestor, also named Edward, tried to rescue Charles I from imprisonment in Carisbrooke Castle.

Gatcombe has some fine stone and thatched cottages and there is also a particularly good example of timber framing. On the right in the middle of the hamlet is the former parish hall, now converted into a private house. The lane ends with tracks going off in several directions, none fit for cars but providing interesting walks.

GODSHILL (F)

For many visitors, Godshill, on the Newport to Shanklin road, represents the perfect example of an English country village: the stereotype of countless postcards and chocolate boxes. It has all the essential ingredients; the church on the hill, curio shops, thatched cottages, an old smithy and afternoon teas in flower-filled gardens (*also see colour section*). For those wishing to take a longer look at what the village has to offer, it is best to visit in winter, when the crowds have gone.

The east end of the village is a good place to start. There you will find, opposite a large car park, the stone-built pub, The Griffin, with the lord of the manor's crest over the door. Next to the car park is a plain but nonetheless attractive Methodist chapel, built in 1838 and still in use as a place of worship today. The main street is lined

Gatcombe Park.

on both sides with shops and tea rooms. On the left is the Model Village, whose miniature attractions happily appeal to all ages.

All Saints' Church is best approached up Church Hollow, which has a fine collection of stone and thatch cottages: the first on the right was formerly the Bell Inn. The earliest surviving parts of the church date from the 14th century with many additions in subsequent periods. The rare double nave probably

Godshill, the Model Village.

hints at its original ownership by Carisbrooke Priory: one nave was for the monks, the other for the villagers. Inside, opposite the entrance, is a painting of the Rubens' school depicting Daniel in the lion's den. It was given to the church by the 1st Earl of Yarborough in the early 19th century and had been in the collection of paintings at Appuldurcombe House, whose ruins, maintained by English Heritage and open to the public for much of the year, are to the south of the village (*see* Wroxall). In St Stephen's Chapel is the church's most celebrated memorial, a rare 15th century wall painting showing Christ crucified on a triple-branched flowering lily, The Lily Cross. The lily is symbolic of the purity of Christ and only a handful of Lily Crosses survive. That at Godshill was over-painted with limewash at the Reformation and subsequently rediscovered and restored in 1966.

The church also contains many fine memorials to the Worsley family, who were lords of the manor and had a large

Godshill. The 15th century wall painting of the Lily Cross.

Godshill. Thatched cottages on the lane leading up to the parish church.

estate nearby. In the north transept is the tomb of Sir Robert Worsley (died 1747) who had started to rebuild the family home at Appuldurcombe; whilst behind the organ is the massive 30 ton sarcophagus of Sir Richard Worsley (died 1805), traveller and collector, who wrote the first history of the Island (1781), and which originally stood in the middle of the church.

Another family with an impressive tomb is the carved Caen stone of Sir John Leigh (died 1529) and his wife, whose effigies lie beneath a canopy arch; Lady Leigh with a shoulder-length headdress, Sir John with his feet resting on a wild boar – he died after falling from his horse whilst boar hunting. The carved monks, or bedesmen, represent the 'Weepers' who prayed for the souls of the dead. On leaving the church, pause for a moment to take in the wonderful view over the village.

Down School Hollow, opposite the junction with School Road, is the old primary school. There has been a school on this site for more than 400 years and, as a plaque over the door states, it was founded before 1615 and rebuilt in 1836 by the Earl of Yarborough: the earl had inherited Appuldurcombe through his marriage to Sir Richard Worsley's niece. Next door to the old primary school is an attractive stone-built schoolhouse.

The surrounding area is good walking country; for example the path north to Great Budbridge or south through Godshill Park towards Wroxall.

GUNVILLE (E)

Now a residential area of Newport, it was first noted in the 18th century and was then merely a group of cottages. It expanded in the early part of the 20th century when a large brickworks opened. It is now closed, and the area consists of housing and retail warehouses. In the main street is a Methodist chapel of 1907, and still in use. From Gunville it is a short distance to Parkhurst Forest.

GURNARD (A)

Once a Roman port and now a village south west of Cowes, and best seen when approaching from its larger neighbour.

On the left is All Saints' Church. Built of yellow and red brick with stone dressings, it opened in 1893 and replaced the Mission Church, erected in Church Road in 1863.

Worsley Road has some interesting houses, varying in size and age, and is well laid out with flower beds and grass edging. It was hereabouts that a failed attempt was made in the late 1850s to develop a garden village. Plots were offered and a brickmaker moved in and opened a yard. Little interest was shown, but the width of Solent View Road and Worsley Road are indicative of the intention to build substantial villas.

From the end of Worsley Road you

Gurnard. The mouth of the Luck stream.

Gurnard. Looking across the Solent from the Esplanade.

can reach the shore and Esplanade – with its beach huts, café and an open space for children. The Esplanade continues east as the Prince's Esplanade, rounding Egypt Point to Cowes. (The origin of the name 'Egypt Point' is not known; it was first recorded in 1771 as Egypt Cliff.) On the left is Solent View Road, which leads to Gurnard Marsh. Although now largely built over, there is a stream called the Luck that flows out to sea.

HAMSTEAD (E)

To the north of Shalfleet, on the western side of the Newtown River, is Hamstead, a private estate purchased in 1806 for about £30,000 by the architect John Nash (*also see* East Cowes). Nash converted a lodge into a picturesque cottage *orné* with a thatched roof and

round tower. The estate was farmed and brickyards and lime kilns were opened, served by a light railway. After Nash's death in 1835 his widow moved to Hamstead from East Cowes Castle, to live with her relations – the Pennethorne family. The estate stayed in their hands until 1923. Nash's cottage has long gone and has been replaced by a more modern house.

The surrounding area consists of plantations of trees and fields, and is best approached on foot along the main drive from the Shalfleet to Yarmouth road. There is an excellent circular walk taking in Hamstead Point, where there is a concrete slipway used to land tanks in the Second World War, and then across to Lower Hamstead and on to rejoin the main drive. The route offers a wide range of views, from forestry to coast to wide open fields – and all the time a sense of peace and quiet. Although the area remains private, the footpaths and lanes are rights of way. From Hamstead there is a coastal path above Bouldnor Cliff and through Bouldnor Copse, and on to Yarmouth – again through a quiet wild landscape.

HAVENSTREET (F)

Just off the slower, but more attractive, road between Ryde and Newport is Havenstreet. Now best known as the home of the Isle of Wight Steam Railway, it was, until the mid 19th century, merely a hamlet with a few

Hamstead Point.

farms and cottages.

In 1852 the Church of St Peter, designed by a Ryde architect, was built, encouraging some development. The railway station – on the Ryde-Newport line – was opened at the southern end of the village in 1875, but the greatest change came seven years later when John Rylands (1801-1888), a Lancashire cotton manufacturer whose works were the largest in Britain and whose investment in the Manchester Ship Canal only added to his wealth, purchased Beaulieu House, near the station. The house was greatly enlarged, renamed Longford House (it is now Northbrooke House), and became Rylands' holiday home. Rylands was a generous philanthropist: the John Rylands University Library, Manchester, is his most spectacular memorial. More modestly, in Havenstreet he built the Longford Institute of 1885 (now Holmdale House) to provide a reading room and leisure facilities for the villagers. Rylands also had a gas works constructed in the railway yard (the retort house of 1886 bears his monogram), and laid piped drinking water to his properties and the workers' cottages.

Most visitors are brought here by the Isle of Wight Steam Railway, whose base is at Havenstreet. The station building is Southern Railway of 1926, and there is a café, shop and museum. The railway is run by volunteers, and is rightly popular with both visitors and islanders alike. It offers rides on steam-hauled trains along 5 miles of track west to Wootton or east to Smallbrook Junction, where there is an interchange with the Island Line electric trains from Shanklin to Ryde Pier Head, and a further link by high speed catamaran to Portsmouth. Many of the restored engines (three of which carry Island place names) and carriages, which are particularly attractive, worked on the Island in the age of steam. The oldest carriage dates to 1864, whilst a locomotive of 1877 is only a dozen years younger (*also see colour section*).

On the hill above the village is a memorial to the men of Binstead and Havenstreet who lost their lives in both World Wars, and nearby is Firestone Copse. This woodland area has many well-marked paths, some of which lead down to Wootton Creek, and plenty of parking. Every spring there is a stunning display of wild daffodils.

Havenstreet. A train of the Isle of Wight Steam Railway arriving from Smallbrook.

Brief Geological History

MARTIN MUNT

The Isle of Wight has a rich diversity of geology. Broadly, the Island can be divided into two: the north is underlain by Palaeogene rocks and the south by Cretaceous rocks. These are divided by the central ridge of Chalk. On the face of it, the Island looks like a slightly buckled layer cake of sedimentary rocks, but these layers mask faults and folds lying below.

THE EARLY CRETACEOUS: 130 – 99.6 million years
The Isle of Wight dinosaurs are found in the rocks called the Wealden Group. These rocks consist of red/purple coloured mudstones, sandstones, lignite beds and gravels. They are thought to have formed as flood deposits and waterlogged soils. Grey coloured layers, called plant-debris beds, are the principal source of dinosaur remains. The climate is believed to have consisted of wet and dry seasons. Rivers fringed with forests of pine, cycads and tree ferns cut through a low-lying landscape. Wildfires swept through the forests, whilst seasonal rains gathered up the dead trees and dinosaurs, dumping them into festering piles; these would later form the plant-debris beds.

About 125 million years ago sea level rises caused the formation of a lagoon, where layers of shale, limestone and sandstone were deposited. The lagoon was home to countless numbers of cockle-like shells called *Filosina*. The layers of paper-thin shales are lined with ostracods, fish bones, bivalves and gastropods. Occasionally, storms would rip-up the cockle-beds and dump them down, eventually forming distinctive shelly limestones. By 120 million years ago the ever-rising sea had flooded the lagoon.

The next 50 million years saw a steady deepening of the sea (called the Cretaceous Marine Transgression), as the Earth went into a period of 'greenhouse' style warming. Shallow, warm coastal waters replaced the lagoon. Sand and mud were deposited, these formed the rocks we call the Lower Greensand Group. This includes the Ferruginous Sands Formation, producing the orange-red cliffs at Lake. The sea was rich with life, including bivalves, ammonites, corals, lobsters and marine reptiles such as Ichthyosaurs. Among the ammonites are hook-shaped *Tropaeum* and *Australiceras*. The overlying Sandrock Formation and Carstone were deposited in a similar setting to the Ferruginous Sands Formation. The Sandrock and Carstone Formation are not particularly rich in fossils. However, plant fossils are common south of Shanklin.

The Lower Greensand Group is overlain by the Gault Clay and Upper Greensand. The Gault Clay represents deep water, the Upper Greensand shallow marine waters. On the Island, both contain only a limited range of fossils, principally, worms, ammonites and bivalves. Toward the top of the Upper Greensand, layers of chert are seen. These indicate the development of sponge forests on the sea floor.

THE LATE CRETACEOUS: 99 – 70 million years
The Chalk Group, which forms the rolling downland scenery, were deposited between 99 and 65 million years ago. It represents the peak of the Cretaceous Marine Transgression, with a deep sea covering much of Northern Europe. Chalk is formed from the accumulation of countless billions of tiny shells called coccoliths.

The Chalk is rich in fossils, notably echinoids, ammonites, belemnites, sponges and bivalves. The Chalk is divided into the Grey Chalk and White Chalk Formations. The White Chalk Formation is characterised by pure limestones (chalk) with layers of flint. The Grey Chalk Formation comprises of calcareous sandstones and limestones.

Locally the youngest part of the Chalk is about 74 million years old; the subsequent 10–11 million years of Chalk deposits were subsequently eroded away and Palaeogene rocks rest unconformably upon it.

THE PALAEOGENE: 58 – 30 million years
By the start of the Palaeogene, the dinosaurs on land and the ammonites in the sea, were among the many life forms that disappeared. Locally, throughout most of the Cretaceous, land had existed over what is now the northern part of the Island, by the Late

Cretaceous this had also become sea. By the Early Palaeogene, the southern part of the Island had probably become land, as rocks were now only forming to the north of the Chalk downs.

The oldest Palaeogene (Palaeocene, Eocene and Oligocene) deposits on the Island are gravels infilling the potholed surface of the Chalk. These are overlain by Reading Clay, a red and purple mottled mud, laid down as soils. The marine rocks of the Thames Group (London Clay), Bracklesham Group and Barton Group follow on. There were occasional brackish and freshwater influences, recorded by layers of the Bournemouth Group extending in from the west. The Thames, Bracklesham and Barton Groups contain a wealth of shellfish indicating sub-tropical conditions.

The coloured sands at Alum Bay derive their colours from the different minerals contained on or between the sand grains. A very wide range of colours are seen in this sequence, which comprises the Thames, Bracklesham, Bournemouth and Barton Groups. One interesting layer, the 'Pipe Clay' (Bournemouth Group), contains beautifully preserved leaf impressions; these include both temperate and sub-tropical forms, such as ginseng, laurel and ferns.

By 37 million years ago when the Solent Group was deposited, the Solent Basin was beginning to fill up. The Solent Group represents a mosaic of different environments such as brackish lagoons and channels, freshwater lakes and ponds, marshes and shallow estuaries. Fossils are abundant and include shellfish, fish, reptiles and mammals. Reptiles include turtles and alligator. Mammals were very diverse and include lemurs, hedgehogs, tapir-like *Palaeotheres* and pig-like *Anthracotheres*. Their remains are common, as are coprolites (fossil dung). By approximately 28 million years ago a tongue of marine water entered the Solent Basin and the youngest parts of the sequence, the Cranmore Member was deposited.

THE NEOGENE: 30 – 2 million years

There is now a gap of about 27 million years. During that time mountain building began in Southern Europe extending throughout Northern Europe as the Alps formed. The movement was sufficient to cause the rocks to fold into their

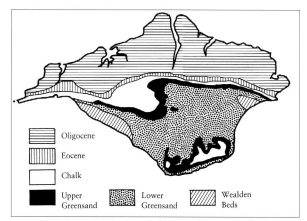

▤	Oligocene
▥	Eocene
☐	Chalk
■	Upper Greensand

| | Lower Greensand | | Wealden Beds |

A geological map of the Island showing the main beds.

present positions, the northern part of the Island being uplifted during the process. About two million years ago the Earth slipped into a pattern of successive periods of extreme cooling and re-heating called the Ice Ages (the Quaternary). On the Island this is marked by gravel terraces, rock debris called Coombe Rock, and peats and muds in the estuaries. Most of these deposits are devoid of fossils. The notable exception is the Last Interglacial (c. 125,000 years ago) mammal fauna found at Newtown on the north-west coast. This contains bison, hippo and straight-tusked elephant.

The last 10,000 years has seen a warming of the Northern Hemisphere and rapid sea level rise. The rising seas have eroded back the rocks of the Isle of Wight at about one metre per year. This erosion, although a threat to the land we live on, is the source of the many exciting discoveries made over the years and the promise of things to come.

A dinosaur footprint near Hanover Point.

HULVERSTONE (E)

A hamlet on the road between Mottistone and Brook. It has a small, stone-built manor house, an old school building – now a private house – a former toll-house, the old Sun Inn, and a few cottages of different coloured stone. On the south side of the hamlet is Hulverstone Lane, which can be the start of a pleasant circular walk through to the Military Road, and back via Downton Cottage and Hulverstone Plantation.

KINGSTON (H)

This peaceful parish – on the Chale to Shorwell road – is the smallest on the Island and comprises undulating arable countryside, a church, manor house and a few cottages.

In the early spring, visitors are greeted by a vivid display of daffodils on a bank near the Church of St Paul. Now closed, the church was built in the 13th century as the church to the manor and largely restored in 1872. It is reached via a path on the right of the farm lane, which joins the main road on the left just before the church.

A few yards along the road is the manor house, which is best viewed from the back of the church. Kingston Manor House is one of the oldest domestic buildings in the Island, still retaining much of its 13th century form. Alterations were carried out in the 17th century, adding to the interest of the building. One of the principal features is the massive old chimney breast, with its five blind brick arches and stacks. Until recently it was the home of the Mew family, who owned it from the early 15th century. This is a private house and not open to the public.

LAKE (G)

What was described as a pretty village in Victorian times is now the residential link between Sandown and Shanklin.

The stone-built Church of the Good Shepherd in Sandown Road was built in 1892 and has a plain interior, notable only for the fact that it has two aisles. Nearby is the former Methodist Chapel, standing behind its modern replacement, which is sited in the main road.

Rather surprisingly, given the proximity of two large seaside towns, Lake still supports a parade of shops and it is near them, in Lake Green Road, that the visitor can see what remains of what was once a large common, and which is still attractive, with plenty of trees and a stream. At the

Kingston Manor House.

far end there is a selection of footpaths leading to the surrounding countryside.

On the road to Newport is the Isle of Wight Airport, from where it is possible to take pleasure flights over much of the Island.

LUCCOMBE (J)

Once a farm, chapel, and a few fishermen's cottages on a ledge in the Chine. Late in the 19th century the cottages had to be abandoned due to coastal erosion, finally disappearing in a 1910 landslip. Because it was lonely and hard to reach, with a steep descent, the Chine was popular with smugglers, who could easily hide their ill-gotten liquor. Even today, the well-wooded valley retains much of its charm (*see colour section*).

In the late 1920s plans were drawn up for a garden village at Luccombe with around 11 building plots offered for sale from £105 each. A plan published in a 1932 sales guide shows the layout of roads and that around 19 houses had already been built. Subsidence meant that some of those have subsequently disappeared, but further building did take place on more solid ground.

The village is best approached from Shanklin along Luccombe Road and the village lies at the end on the right-hand side. From the road the coastal path continues on its way to Bonchurch past the path down to Luccombe Chine, unfortunately now closed following a landslip.

MERSTONE (F)

The soil around this attractive hamlet in the Arreton Valley is extremely fertile, and this has made it a notable centre for horticulture: its name derives from 'a farm in the marsh'. The main road is lined with cottages of various ages and at the south end, on the west side, is what remains of the former railway station, Merstone Junction (closed in 1956). The site is now a car park and is a good starting place for a walk through the mainly flat but nevertheless pleasant surrounding countryside.

Mottistone Manor, once the home of the Seely family and now owned by the National Trust.

The only other road is Chapel Lane, an attractive side road that contains the red brick Methodist chapel of 1848. Farther along is Broadfields Farm, whose owners have grown vegetables in the area for more than 100 years. Thanks to a right of way it is possible to get a look at the attractive 17th-century manor house. While most Island manor houses are of stone construction, Merstone is brick-built with stone dressings. Its situation provides some fine views north to nearby St George's Down, and south across the valley.

MOTTISTONE (E)

The hamlet is positioned around a small but unspoilt green and lies in front of the manor house. Mottistone – on the road from Brighstone to Brook – has a few stone built cottages, a parsonage, manor farm and a church. It also has one of the most attractive manor houses on the Isle of Wight, which sits snugly against the steep bank of Mottistone Down (*also see colour section*).

The manor came into the hands of the Cheke family in the 14th century, when Thomas Cheke commanded the local militia. In due course Thomas's successors built the present manor house in two phases. To Robert Cheke

(died 1500) we owe the east wing, which was built in the late 15th century and probably incorporates at least some of the original Saxon house. His grandson, Thomas, transformed the early Tudor house into a much larger Elizabethan one by adding the west wing, which is set at right angles to its predecessor, completing the work by adding his initials and the date 1567 to the new porch. The best known of the Cheke's is Thomas's cousin, Sir John Cheke (1514-1557), tutor to the young Edward VI, but who was later sent to the Tower for foolishly involving himself in the plot to put Lady Jane Grey on the throne after Edward's death in 1553. Forced to renounce Protestantism to avoid being burnt at the stake by Queen Mary, he died a broken man, carrying 'God's pardon and all good men's pity'. Within 70 years Mottistone had been sold, initially to Robert Dillington of Knighton Gorges.

In 1703 a storm caused the light sandy soil on the hillside behind the house to engulf the back of it with over a thousand tons of earth. The manor house became a farmhouse until 1861 when the entire estate was purchased by a wealthy Nottinghamshire coal-owner, Charles Seely (1803-1887), for £28,000 (*see* Brook). His son Charles (1833-1915) was a great benefactor to the Island, giving £5,000, plus £100 a year towards the running costs, to the Isle of Wight County Council to provide a public library service: he was created a baronet in 1896.

Sir Charles's second son, Jack (1868-1947) inherited the Brook and Mottistone estates in 1915. He served with great distinction as a cavalry officer in both the Boer and First World Wars. He became a General, M.P. for the Isle of Wight, and coxswain of the Brook Lifeboat (he had first joined its crew aged 17). He was Lord Lieutenant of Hampshire and the Wight for thirty years from 1917; and in 1933 was created the 1st Lord Mottistone. In 1924 he decided to move his home from Brook House to Mottistone Manor, still buried up to the eaves at the back with earth. The restoration of the house and the removal of the landslip was supervised by his architect son, John, later the 2nd Lord Mottistone, who died in 1963 and bequeathed most of the estate to the National Trust.

The house is now occupied by Sir Charles Nicholson, a relation to the Seely family and is open to the public on

Mottistone. The Long Stone is all that remains of a Neolithic long barrow and is situated on the Down behind the manor house.

Jack Seely, later 1st Lord Mottistone, when a crew member of the Brook Lifeboat.

August Bank Holiday Monday. The gardens, however, are open from spring to autumn. Opposite are a pretty village green and a small cemetery, which contains the graves of many of the occupants of the manor house. It also contains the grave of an unknown sailor from the First World War.

The adjoining church of St Peter and St Paul was originally built in the 12th century, although what survives today is mainly 15th century – along with later improvements. The wooden boards lining the chancel roof came from the 1862 wreck of the barque *Cedarine*, in which many of the 100 who drowned were ex-convicts returning from Bermuda to freedom after serving their sentence.

On the north side of the chancel is the manorial chapel built in the 15th century by Robert Cheke. The ashes of the 1st Lord Mottistone lie in front of the altar, and the 2nd is commemorated by a stone within the sanctuary. On the north side of the chancel is a table-tomb of Lady Jane Dillington, who died in 1674. It is also claimed that she is buried at Newchurch, in which parish lies Knighton House, principal seat of the Dillington family. The fine Jacobean pulpit is spoilt by being placed on a modern stone base.

Just off the road to the west of the village is the National Trust car park, a handy starting place for a number of

walks. One favourite route begins on the left of the manor house and continues up on to the Downs, passing on the way a wooded area, which is spectacularly carpeted by bluebells in spring. The path reaches the Long Stone, the larger of two stones that are all that remains of an ancient Neolithic long barrow. It is thought that the stone served as the Saxon 'moot', or 'meet' stone, hence the name of the village. From the summit of Mottistone Down there are glorious views over the Back of the Wight.

THE NEEDLES (D)

The chalk stacks at the western end of the Island are amongst the most iconic of all British images – as famous and as photographed as Dover's white cliffs. They are the last vestiges of when the Isle of Wight was joined to the mainland, and get their name from a 120 feet high slender pinnacle rock known as Lot's Wife that fell in 1772 through erosion, and whose stump can still be seen at low tide.

Following a number of shipwrecks and complaints by shipowners, the first lighthouse was built by Trinity House on the downs above the Needles in 1785. It was 143m (470ft) above sea level and the light had a range of 17.7km (11 miles). Because of its height above the sea the light was often shrouded in sea mist and of limited use to mariners.

Despite its poor quality, this rare stereoscopic view of the Needles is the only known photograph to show the building of the present Needles lighthouse in 1858-59.

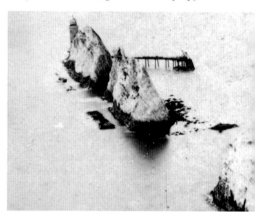

The Needles. An engraving showing the pinnacle rock, known as Lot's Wife, which fell in 1772.

RIGHT *The Needles lighthouse today with its heliport on the top.*

In 1859 Trinity House built a new lighthouse near sea level on the outermost of the chalk rocks. The base of the rock was cut away with dynamite to form the foundations and store-houses were excavated in the chalk. The granite for the building of the lighthouse was brought by ship into Totland Bay, where it was dressed and cut, before being shipped to the site of the lighthouse and unloaded at a jetty built alongside the foundations. The new light commenced operating on 1st January 1859. The cost was £20,000 (over £1.5 million today). The present light has a range of 17 miles and is fully automated.

NETTLESTONE (G)

Although now regarded as part of Seaview, Nettlestone has managed to retain its own identity and is centred on a small but attractive green. On the road to Ryde is a row of interesting red-brick houses whose mock timber framing is really cement moulded and coloured to resemble timber. The houses were designed by the local architect Stephen Salter in the 1890s and are named after universities and public schools – Oxford, Cambridge, Rugby, Eton, Harrow, Marlborough, Radley and Winchester.

Farther along the road is an interesting manor house (private). Built of brick on a stone plinth between 1550-1600, it is thought to be the oldest brick building on the Island. The large chimney stack was probably added in the late 16th century.

NEWBRIDGE (E)

On the road from Calbourne to Yarmouth, near where it crosses the Caul Bourne. The village has a number of brick and stone cottages and, on the south side of the road, the old Primitive Methodist Chapel, which was bought by the parish in 1960 for monthly services and is now a private house. Further up the hill on the north side is a

Nettlestone. Mock-timber framed houses on the road to Ryde.

Newbridge. The old school, now the Community Centre.

Newchurch. The gate posts on the drive which once led to Knighton Gorges House.

large caravan park and beyond, on the same side, is the local Working Men's Club, first formed in 1908, and now Newbridge Community Centre. The stone part of the building was the former infant school, although there is a recent extension. To the north, beside the Caul Bourne is Lower Calbourne Mill. This now disused mill can be seen from a right of way, which passes close by on its way to Shalfleet.

Newchurch. The Church of All Saints with its distinctive wooden clad tower.

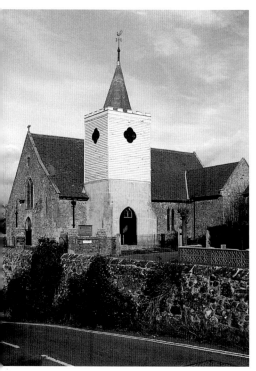

NEWCHURCH (F)

Approach the village from the north, along the Downs Road, and take in the magnificent panoramic views over the valley to the downs in the south of the Island. An attractive lane leads down into the valley and the hamlet of Langbridge, which consists of a large house, cottages and a small chapel. Beyond this is the causeway over the River Yar, from where the road climbs the hill into Newchurch.

The centre of this historically important village is disappointing. Many of the old cottages have been destroyed and replaced by uninteresting 19th and 20th century houses.

On the left is All Saints' Church, one of the six original parishes endowed to the Norman Abbey of Lyre by William Fitz Osborn in the 11th century. It is possible that he ordered the replacement of an existing Saxon church, giving the village its name in the process.

Much of what we can see today dates from the 13th century and, until the mid 19th century, the vast parish of Newchurch stretched across the Island from Ryde beach to Ventnor shore. The spire and the wooden boarded tower, which is lit at night, can be seen for miles across the valley. From the churchyard, which contains a fine 17th century sundial, are splendid views to the north.

Once inside the church, the eye is drawn to the soaring chancel arch and the roof timbers, which were exposed when the plaster ceiling was removed in 1883. The vestry in the north transept was originally a chantry, but is now lined with memorials to the Dillington family, who lived at Knighton Gorges manor house, to the north of the village.

If Knighton Gorges had not been deliberately demolished by its owner it would surely be one of the most important houses on the Island. One historian, writing shortly before it's demolition in 1821, described it as 'by far the most considerable and beautiful of the ancient mansions of the Island'. The house was situated under the south side of Ashey Down, in a sheltered site with views across the valley to the south of the Island. Engravings show a substantial Elizabethan manor overlooking a lake.

In the 12th century the manor was owned by the Morvilles, of whom Hugh was one of the murderers of Thomas à Becket in Canterbury Cathedral. In 1563 it was bought by the Dillington family, who rebuilt the house. Legend has it that in 1721 Sir Tristram Dillington committed suicide by drowning in the lake.

In 1765 the manor came into the possession of Maurice George Bisset, who made the house the centre of fashionable society on the Island. A few years later he eloped with the wife of Sir Richard Worsley of Appuldurcombe (*see* Wroxall), a cause of much scandal at the time, and the house was in poor condition by Bisset's death in 1821.

Newport. Carisbrooke Road, Alexandra Terrace with its raised pavement.

Newchurch. The Garlic Fair is held annually to raise funds for the benefit of the village.

There are two versions of what happened next. In one he willed it to his brother, William Bisset, who sold the house and the rest of the estate to Sir Samuel Spicer, of Portsmouth, for £45,000, who later demolished the house. The second version is the more dramatic. Supposedly, it was George Bisset's daughter's determination to marry a clergyman her father disapproved of that caused the house's destruction. Bissett swore that if his daughter married she would never set foot in the house. She went ahead. Bissett moved into a cottage shortly before his death and ordered Knighton Gorges' demolition. Sadly, this much embroidered legend is untrue, but what is true is that all that is left of Knighton Gorges are a pair of stone gate posts beside the Newchurch–Ashey Down road (map ref: 565871).

In School Lane is the public car park, opposite the greatly enlarged village school. Newchurch is well blessed with public halls; the community hall in the school, the parish hall next to the church and the village hall in the main street. At the south end of the village is the former local shop, now a private house, notable for the spectacular May-flowering wisteria that covers its frontage. Outside is a restored milestone informing passers-by that London lies 91 miles away.

In the summer the village hosts a garlic fair (garlic is grown extensively locally), which has proved popular with visitors and Islanders alike. There are several good walks in the area, including the cycle path, which can be joined at Langbridge. From here you can walk towards Newport or, in the opposite direction, Sandown.

NEWPORT (F)

The Island's 'capital' and market town lies at the centre of the county and at the head of the navigable River Medina. Nearby is Carisbrooke Castle, historically the Island's defence headquarters. In short, Newport is ideally suited to its important role in the life of the Isle of Wight.

The Lord of the Isle of Wight, Richard de Redvers, laid out the gridiron street pattern that can still be seen today in the late 12th century. Originally a 'New Port' for Carisbrooke, it was not until the 18th century and the onset of the Napoleonic wars that the town began to grow and prosper. Sir John Oglander thought it a 'poor sort of place', its development having been held back by the Black Death in 1348, a fire started by French invaders in 1377 and a second outbreak of plague in 1584.

The town still contains some fine 18th century town houses and its charms were noted by Henry Wyndham in his 1794 guide to the Isle of Wight: 'Newport is a handsome and well built town, the shops are numerous, and as superbly stocked as they are in most of the English cities'. His description could as easily apply to the 21st century town. Newport has continued to grow, and though no longer a port of any significance it is now the main centre for shopping on the Island, as well as providing the headquarters for the Isle of Wight Council.

A walking tour of the town should begin in Carisbrooke Road (south end of the High Street). Here is the finest mall (raised pavement) on the Island, consisting of a wide pavement lined with trees and backed by the splendid Alexandra Terrace. Built in the mid 19th century as a terrace of houses, they are now mainly offices.

Unfortunately, there was rather too much heavy-handed redevelopment of

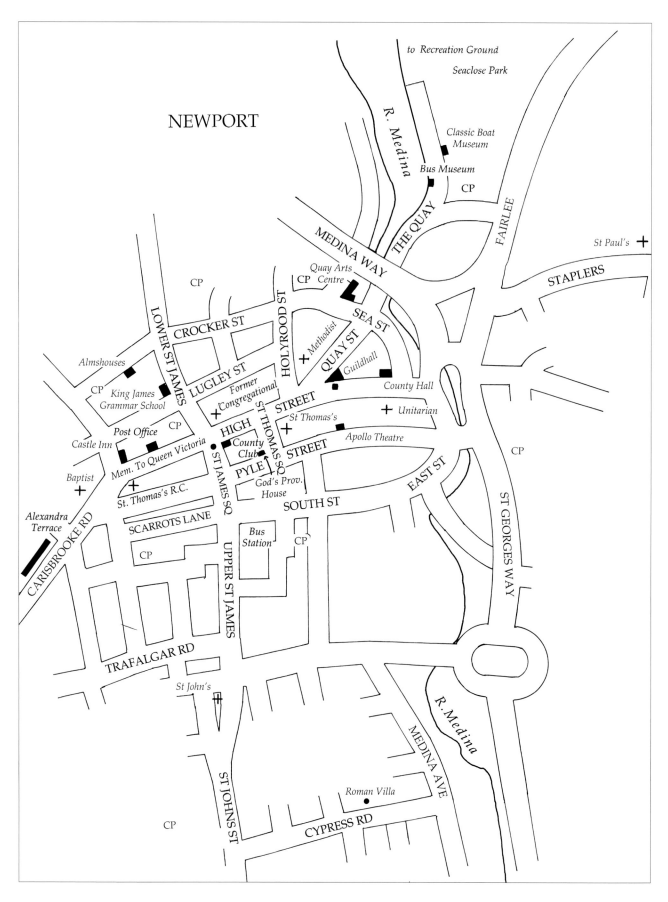

NEWPORT

to Recreation Ground

Seaclose Park

R. Medina

Classic Boat Museum

Bus Museum

CP

FAIRLEE

St Paul's

STAPLERS

MEDINA WAY

THE QUAY

Quay Arts Centre

CP

CP

CROCKER ST

LOWER ST JAMES

HOLYROOD ST

SEA ST

Methodist

QUAY ST

Guildhall

County Hall

Almshouses

LUGLEY ST

CP

King James Grammar School

Former Congregational

ST THOMAS ST

STREET

St Thomas's

Unitarian

Post Office

CP

HIGH

Castle Inn

Mem. To Queen Victoria

County Club

PYLE

Apollo Theatre

STREET

Baptist

ST JAMES SQ

St. Thomas's R.C.

God's Prov. House

SOUTH ST

EAST ST

ST GEORGES WAY

CP

Alexandra Terrace

CARISBROOKE RD

SCARROTS LANE

CP

Bus Station

CP

UPPER ST JAMES

R. Medina

TRAFALGAR RD

St John's

MEDINA AVE

ST JOHNS ST

Roman Villa

CP

CYPRESS RD

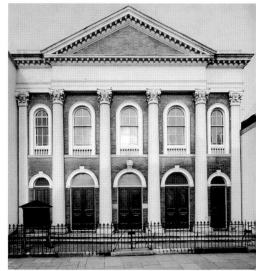

Newport in the 1950s and 1960s, and many of the old town houses in the High Street have been destroyed or altered out of all recognition. One has survived – next to the Post Office at the west end of the High Street is one of Newport's older buildings, the small red brick-built Castle Inn, dated 1684. Nearby is an imposing Baptist Chapel of 1809, enlarged in 1872.

Head east down the High Street and you will see the large memorial to Queen Victoria, designed by Percy Stone, a local architect, and unveiled by Princess Beatrice, the Queen's youngest daughter, in 1903. Close by is a monument to Earl Mountbatten of Burma, Governor of the Isle of Wight and, from 1974 until his death five years later at the hands of the IRA, the Island's first Lord Lieutenant – and after whom the Lord Louis Library in Orchard Street is named. Behind is St James's Square, formerly the cattle market, and next to the monument is the Isle of Wight County Club, a stone

ABOVE LEFT *Newport. The town suffered from post war development with several town houses and streets being cleared. This 1970s photograph of Sea Street shows that it largely avoided demolition: only the three storey house with the flat roof house has gone.*

ABOVE *Newport. The elegant frontage of the Baptist Chapel.*

BELOW *Newport. St. James's Square. The tall column is a memorial to Queen Victoria, the short one in the centre is a monument to Earl Mountbatten.*

Newport. A 1960s photograph of John Nash's Guildhall, now the Museum of Island History.

Newport. These disused warehouses were converted into the popular Quay Arts Centre.

building with five open arches at street level that was the work of the architect John Nash and was built in 1819 as a literary institution and reading room.

Farther along the High Street is more evidence of Nash's handiwork on the Island, the classical style Guildhall with its colonnade and Ionic portico. Built in 1818, the clock tower was added in 1887 to mark Queen Victoria's Golden Jubilee. The ground floor was originally intended for the sale of market produce, but was later altered to house the town fire engine. Today the building is the home of the Museum of Island History, which portrays the story of the Isle of Wight from prehistoric times to the present.

Behind the Guildhall is the impressive Quay Street, which contains some interesting houses and the Methodist Chapel of 1880, whose foundation stone was laid by Charles Clifford, the last MP for Newport. The law courts are on the opposite side of the street.

As the name implies, Quay Street leads down to the Quay and the Quay Arts Centre. The centre was opened in 1977 after the conversion of quayside warehouses, and is now a popular and thriving centre which stages a wide variety of events for both adults and children – including antique fairs, art exhibitions, music, cinema and theatre: there is also a gallery space and a café.

The area can serve as the starting point for an excellent walk. Take the eastern side of the river, past the Riverside Centre, on to the Classic Boat Museum

Newport Quay. Coasters no longer tie up alongside, and part of the Quay is now a marina.

and the Isle of Wight Bus Museum. From there, continue to Sea Close Playing Fields and on along the riverbank to the highly popular Folly Inn.

Returning to Newport, at the eastern end of the High Street is County Hall, headquarters of the unitary authority for the Island. Built in the Art Deco style in 1937-38, a less attractive addition was constructed in 1967-69. Opposite County Hall is the Unitarian Chapel of 1774, extended in 1825.

Proceeding along Lower St James's Street, from St James's Square, the first building of interest is the former Congregational Church. This is the third such building on the site and dates back to 1848: its predecessors were built in 1669 and 1777. Farther along is what is probably the oldest building in Newport – the King James Grammar School, erected in 1614. It was here that Charles I, who was imprisoned in Carisbrooke Castle in 1648, met the Parliamentary Commissioners to try and negotiate a treaty (known as the Treaty of Newport).

Close by in Crocker Street are the Worsley Almshouses, which were founded in 1618 by Sir Richard Worsley, in accordance with the will of Giles Kent. They were rebuilt and modernised in 1879, with decorative tiles, porches and leaded windows. Now, as when they were first built, the buildings provide homes for widows from Newport or Godshill. Crocker Street offers a second example of local philanthropy. In a niche over the doorway of number 62 is a replica of 'Blue Jenny' – a carved figure of a girl in school uniform carrying a bible and coin. The figure is a reminder of the Newport Blue School Foundation, a charity school founded in 1761 for the free education of 26 local girls. The school has long since closed, but the charitable foundation still awards bursaries. A turning on the right from the High Street leads into St Thomas's Square, which in previous centuries was the corn market.

In the centre of the Square is the parish church of St Thomas. Although

Newport, Lower St James's Street. King James Grammar School of 1614, probably the oldest building in the town.

the date of the present building is 1854 – the foundation stone was laid by Prince Albert – the first church on the site was built in 1180. Inside is a finely carved pulpit, which was donated to the church in 1631 by the then Mayor of Newport. At the east end of the south aisle is the tomb of Sir Edward Horsey, Captain of the Wight from 1565 to 1582, containing his marble inlaid effigy. Horsey died of plague at Haseley Manor, and history describes him as an

Newport, Crocker Street. The replica of 'Blue Jenny'.

Newport, St Thomas's Church. The pulpit presented by the mayor in 1631.

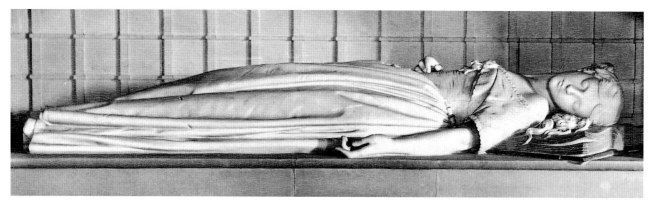

ABOVE *Newport, St Thomas's Church, the Carrera marble memorial to Princess Elizabeth, who died aged 15 in 1650 and is buried in the church.*

LEFT *Newport, St Thomas's Church, the tomb of Sir Edward Horsey.*

Nearby, in Church Litten, is another reminder of the plague in the form of the burial ground which had to be hastily opened to cope with the numbers of dead. The Tudor archway and a few of the memorials still stand, while the surroundings have been turned into a small public park. One of the memorials is to Valentine Gray, a chimney sweep, aged 9, who was found dead in an outhouse in 1822. His employer was sent to prison.

able military commander who was not above being involved in piracy and privateering (*see* Arreton). Princess Elizabeth, second daughter of Charles I, is buried beneath the chancel. She died at Carisbrooke Castle, aged 15, of a chill, having been caught in a shower of rain on the Castle bowling green; and her lead casket was discovered by workmen in 1793 under the old chancel floor. The Princess, together with her brother, Henry, Duke of Gloucester, had been summoned to the Island following the death of their father. On completion of the present building, Queen Victoria commissioned Baron Marochetti to carve a memorial in Carrera marble to the princess 'as a token of respect for her virtues, and of sympathy for her misfortunes', and it now stands in the north chapel.

Behind the church is God's Providence House, now a tea room and restaurant and one of Newport's most interesting town houses. This lovely brick-built house was erected in 1701 on the site of an earlier house. According to the town records it was here that, in 1584, thanks to 'God's Providence', the plague stopped spreading.

In Lower Pyle Street is the Apollo Theatre, originally built as the Methodist Chapel in 1804. It closed in 1969 and was bought by a group of

LEFT *Newport, Church Litten. This Tudor archway was the entrance to the old burial ground, now an open grass space.*

RIGHT *Newport, Church Litten. A memorial to a nine-year-old chimney sweep found dead in an outhouse in 1822, and buried in the old cemetery.*

Newtown. The old Town Hall of 1700 dates back to when Newtown was a 'Rotten Borough' sending two MPs to Parliament.

volunteers who converted it into what is now a popular and well-supported local theatre. At the western end of Pyle Street is the late 18th century Church of St Thomas of Canterbury, the oldest Roman Catholic church to be built on the Island.

In Cypress Road on the outskirts of Newport are the remains of a Roman villa, uncovered in 1926 by workmen digging the foundations for a garage. The second century villa consisted of two ranges of rooms linked by a corridor verandah. Of particular note are the bath rooms, which are some of the best preserved in Britain, and have hypocaust heating, and both hot and cold rooms. A local man purchased the site and paid for a cover building to protect the villa beneath. Finally, the site passed into the ownership of the Isle of Wight County Council and in recent years steps have been taken to make a visit more rewarding: it is open to the public throughout spring and summer.

Barton Village, on the eastern side of

Newport, was developed as a residential area for the working population of the town by a builder named Barton and greatly expanded after the Second World War. On the north side of Barton is the Church of St Paul. Stone built and neo-Norman in design, it was erected in 1884 and has some fine stained glass windows.

In the southern part of Newport is the Church of St John, constructed of local stone in 1837, although the weathering of the stone gives it a much older appearance.

NEWTOWN (E)
Colourful stories, Island history, and some of the most unspoilt countryside in the Island give Newtown a charm peculiarly its own.

Founded in the 13th century on land held by the Bishop of Winchester, it was originally named Francheville (free town). Once one of the Island's most important towns and a busy port it was

devastated by fire after the same French raid of 1377 that saw Newport be attacked and never fully recovered. In 1585 Elizabeth I granted Newtown borough status and the right to elect two Members of Parliament. As a 'rotten borough', the two families who controlled the properties carrying votes were still cheerfully nominating an MP each until the Reform Act of 1832. Newtown Creek was once a deep harbour which could take ships up to 500 tons. What remains today are a few cottages, a church, the Town Hall and some empty fields, now all fortunately in the ownership of the National Trust, thus insuring the preservation of this unique area.

The only way to begin to appreciate what happened here is on foot and the place to start is the Town Hall, situated conveniently opposite the National Trust car park. It was built of brick and dressed stone in 1700 on the site of an earlier structure, and is a perfect miniature town hall, with two flights of

ABOVE *Newtown. For many years the local pub, but closed in 1916.*

RIGHT *Newtown. Marsh Farmhouse and the path leading down to the bird hide.*

steps at one end, and round-headed Gothic windows and a little portico at the other. It is open in the summer and a visit is a must for those wishing to understand Newtown's fascinating story. By 1932 the building was in a bad state of repair and was presented to the National Trust in the following year. The cost of restoration and repair was paid for by a group of anonymous benefactors known only by the sobriquet, the Ferguson Gang. A further touch of mystery and romance was provided by the fact that the money was delivered by a masked member of the gang.

A short distance from the Town Hall is an early 18th century house, which was, until 1916, the local pub. The cottage on the corner of the High Street has a Victorian wall letter box, whilst further along, on the left, is the village pump, installed in 1894 and restored by a group of young people as part of a training scheme in 1983. The Church of the Holy Spirit, built in 1835, was designed in the medieval style by a Portsmouth architect and stands on the site of a much older building that had become a ruin.

After the church the High Street turns right and becomes Church Street. On the left is Myrtle Cottage, which contains some unusual brickwork made locally at the Elmsworth brickworks. Before turning left into Key Street, note Marsh Farmhouse with its ornate woodwork. At the end of the street on the right is the former coastguard's cottage, built in the 1860s. Beside it is a path that leads across a field to one of Newtown's key sites, a National Nature Reserve. As well as oyster beds, there was once a salt industry at Newtown. Just before crossing the footbridge the remains of the brick salt-house can be seen on your right, whilst at the far end, on the left, are the flooded salt-pans.

The 288 hectare Newton Harbour National Nature Reserve covers the creeks and marshes and attracts thousands of over-wintering wildfowl and waders. Because it combines ancient woodland, damp meadows and saltmarsh it is also important for wild flowers – many of them rare – and for butterflies. There is the remains of a little quay, and in summer Newtown Creek is a popular anchorage.

Newtown is a fine area for walking. There are many easy walks, not only across the marshes but also in the woods and tracing the routes of long-gone streets.

Newtown. Looking across the meadows and saltmarsh towards the Quay and Creek.

ABOVE *Alum Bay, showing the coloured sands in the cliffs.*

BELOW *Looking north-west from the fort on Bembridge Down.*

ABOVE *Winkle Street, Calbourne.*
RIGHT *North Street, Brighstone.*
BELOW RIGHT *The Town Hall and church, Brading.*
BELOW *Church Hollow, Godshill.*

ABOVE *Carisbrooke Castle.*
RIGHT *Isle of Wight Steam Railway, Ashey.*
BELOW *The Church of St Andrew, Chale.*
BOTTOM *Cowes, East Cowes and the River Medina.*

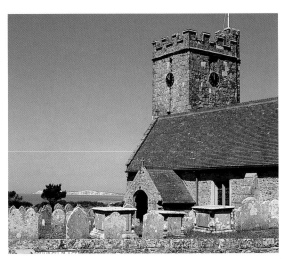

ABOVE *The Needles, Alum Bay and West Wight, with Fort Albert in the distance.*
LEFT *Mottistone Manor.*
BELOW *Luccombe Chine.*
OPPOSITE PAGE TOP *The Guildhall, Newport, with the River Medina in the distance.*
OPPOSITE PAGE BOTTOM *The entrance to the Eastern Gardens, Ryde, with the former Pavilion on the left.*

LEFT *Sandown and Sandown Bay.*
ABOVE *Ventnor, with the Cascade in the foreground.*
BELOW *The Undercliff, looking east near St Lawrence.*

A Naturalist's Paradise

BILL SHEPARD

To enjoy the natural heritage of the Isle of Wight, and there is so much to see, no better investment can be made than in a good map (the Ordnance Survey Explorer Map no. OL 29, 1:25,000 is recommended). This tiny island, with 500 hundred miles of footpaths, habitats of every description, and whose former railways tracks are often now cycle routes following the lush river valleys, is best enjoyed at a leisurely pace. Leave the car behind and delight in the unparalleled scenery for nothing.

With a vegetative covering including some twelve hundred flowering plants it would take you a lifetime to claim familiarity. The habitats of this small place interlock like the pieces of a jigsaw and to experience the same range on the mainland would require traversing the length of the English south coast. For the walker the ever-changing scenery is breathtaking. The treats on offer include summer walks through fern-filled sunken lanes on the greensand; gravelled tracks through mixed woodland on the heavy clay across the north of the Island, where red squirrels watch you pass. Perhaps a winter visit would tempt you to climb the chalk spine of downland across the centre of the Island from east to west, offering breath-taking views and dry walking. There is the Undercliff on the south east coast where the warm climate enables the tenderest of plants to thrive. What about the cliffs of sand or chalk, the latter rising to some six hundred feet? Here the peregrine falcon puts on an aerial display and ravens announce their presence with a deep honking call.

This is an ornithologist's paradise. The three key areas for bird watching, particularly for those interested in waders are: the mouth of the Western Yar River (accessed from Yarmouth); the harbour at the mouth of the Eastern Yar River between St Helens and Bembridge; and the tidal section of the River Medina, where a former railway track (now a cycle route) runs along the eastern bank providing an excellent viewing platform. Any of these places

A bird hide at Newtown Creek.

can contain hundreds of visiting winter birds and a count of fifty species is easily accomplished. The walk between Ryde and Seaview is rewarding for the bird watcher. Tiny sanderlings can be seen advancing and retreating at the shore line like tiny clockwork toys. At Seaview can be seen a variety of divers out at sea and there is also the Hersey Nature Reserve (complete with hide) but as there is a bird park adjacent there can be some very exotic and surprising visitors!

The highlight for the ornithologist must be the Newtown National Nature Reserve. Although a telescope is recommended for the best results the bird watching is generally excellent. The hide is manned throughout the summer months by volunteers willing to share their knowledge. A rarer feathered inhabitant of the Island is the Dartford warbler. This little bird can be seen throughout the year but is particularly evident in spring when nesting. A walk along the chalk ridge from Brighstone to Freshwater Bay and then again on the top of High Down at the western end will usually reveal the bird sitting in the gorse.

If you are with children and they have never seen glow worms then a visit to Mottistone Down (grid ref: 420 845) at dusk is recommended. It is however, important that the glow worms are not disturbed as their numbers have decreased significantly over the last century. July and August are the months of mating when the female attracts her mate with the distinctive fluorescent light. Another special delight for children is the wall lizard. The Le Falaise car park in Ventnor (grid ref: 565 773) is the place to

The backwaters of the River Medina are easily accessible and are an easy way of watching wildfowl and waders.

visit where the morning sun warms the walls and the lizards emerge to soak up the heat. While in Ventnor take the opportunity to visit the Botanic Garden, where the especially mild climate supports many tender plants, such as the banana.

The Forestry Commission plantations across the Island contain both conifer and broadleaf trees and are popular venues for walking for both residents and visitors alike. Firestone Copse at Wootton (grid ref: 558 910) and Parkhurst Forest (grid ref: 481 901) both have good parking facilities. Firestone Copse has a spectacular display of wild daffodils each spring in March. Along the verges of the rides the rare long-leaved lungwort, *Pulmonaria Longifolia* will be seen. This is a national rarity, confined only to the counties in central southern England. The copse stretches down to the edge of Wootton Creek where a path bordering the Creek gives the opportunity for some bird watching. Herons can often be seen.

Parkhurst Forest, which can be accessed from the Newport to Yarmouth road, is an area of some 395 hectares of woodland. The visitor is well advised to keep to the marked paths. A special treat, but only with a guide, is a visit at dusk to hear the nightjars churring and wing-clapping in flight, the roding woodcock with its frog-like call and perhaps the additional bonus of the sight of the long–eared owl in its silent flight.

Other areas of woodland worth visiting include Fort Victoria Country Park (grid ref: 339 896), which has guided walks and magnificent views across the western Solent. Borthwood, an area of National Trust woodland (grid ref: 570 844), is an attractive area of undulating woodland on the greensand. There is some parking off the Apse Heath/Winford road. Godshill Beech Wood (grid ref: 531 812) is accessed via a path which leads off from behind the Griffin public house. A visit to this wood in April will reward you with one of the most beautiful sights of the English countryside, an extensive carpet of bluebells. There is also good public access to the Westover Plantation, with car parking at the foot of Mottistone Down (grid ref: 420 845). Walk up through the woodland to the western extremity and before turning left to reach the summit pause to take in the spectacular view of the West Wight and beyond to the mainland coast. On top of the down are the Harborough ancient burial mounds, and then the return leg to the car is a pleasant downhill stroll. The People's Trust for Endangered Species is responsible for Hurst Copse at Wootton. This area of woodland is dominated by hornbeam, and there is an interesting icehouse close to the entrance.

The Island is noted as a habitat for the red squirrel and any of the woodlands mentioned above contain them. However, it is worth remembering

Dartford Warblers can be seen along the chalk ridge between Brighstone and Freshwater.

that like foxes and badgers they have learned that there are easy meals to be had from gardens, from bird tables. So often red squirrels can be seen in gardens and at tourist attractions such as Osborne House.

Strange as it may seem some of the Island's cemeteries are well worth visiting as they can be important habitats. Northwood Cemetery (grid ref: 494 949 and accessed from Newport Road, Cowes) produces an excellent display of daffodils and crocus in early spring and at all other times a good collection of trees and shrubs. The Freshwater parish churchyard (grid ref: 345 873) is perhaps best described as an arboretum and in close proximity are a country park and a nature reserve. A visit to Carisbrooke Cemetery on Mount Joy (grid ref: 489 878) is an absolute must in the first week of May. Here careful management and conservation has resulted in the most stunning carpet of cowslips. Access is easy, even for those in a car.

The Island is blessed with more than twenty species of wild orchid. Some of the more common varieties are easily spotted, including early purple, bee, common spotted and pyramidal. The Island also has a rare butterfly, the Glanville fritillary, which draws butterfly enthusiasts from across Britain. The coast of the Island is also known for thrift which can be found along the coastal path west of Compton Chine.

Having highlighted some of the rarities to be found on the Island it is important to draw attention to the 'Code of Conduct for the Conservation of Wild Plants'. It is illegal for anyone, without the permission of the owner or occupier of the land, to dig up wild plants. A number of rare species, both flora and fauna are totally protected by law. Perhaps equally compelling among nature lovers is the saying 'leave for others to enjoy'.

A local rarity, the Glanville Fritillary butterfly.

Walk the Island

The Island can be justly proud of its network of footpaths, bridleways and byways, which total over 800 km (500 miles). Given a limited budget the 1,383 individual pathways are well maintained and sign-posted. Anyone wishing to escape the hustle and bustle should take to the rights of way, discovering for themselves all the Island has to offer. Whether on the downland, in the valleys, or on the coast, there are hundreds of wonderful views to be enjoyed.

One of the most popular routes is the Coastal Path which encircles the Island for some 96 km (60 miles). The scenery is diverse, ranging from high chalk cliffs to flat saltings and marsh areas. These paths will be of interest to geologists, ornithologists, botanists, archaeologists and historians – as well as the Sunday afternoon rambler. There is something to interest all.

Those seeking further information on the Coastal Path should visit a Tourist Information Centre to obtain *The Coastal Path and Inland Trails on the Isle of Wight*, a helpful booklet of six coastal path walks and eight inland trails. The Coastal Path is divided into sections ranging from 13 km (8 miles) in length to 26 km (16 miles). The inland trails also vary in length and mainly cover the northern half of the Island, enabling the walker to enjoy a diverse landscape with much woodland. The Downland Way is a popular footpath and bridleway running some 6.5 km (4 miles) from Brading Down westwards to near Dowend, Arreton. Alternatively if you are eager to savour the views the central chalk ridge can be walked from Bembridge Down, in the east, to the western tip of the Island at the Needles, by following the Bembridge and Tennyson Trails.

The local Tourist Information Centres sell various booklets detailing long and short walks. Another way to see the countryside is to cycle some of the specially made paths. There are now several of these cycleways, the longest being from Cowes through to Newport and then on to Sandown. Leaflets on these routes are also available.

A lane from Rowborough Down, near Shorwell.

NINGWOOD (E)

A hamlet on the south side of the Newport-Yarmouth road. At the junction of the main road are the local primary school and the pub while the rest of the hamlet lies along the road to Newbridge.

Proceeding along this road, on the left is the manor house, which up to the Dissolution of the Monasteries, belonged to Christchurch Priory. The manor was seized by the Crown and sold to Thomas Hobson, of London. What can be seen today is a 17th century house with an imposing front added in 1784 by John Pinhorn, a London banker who had been born in Newport.

Further along a left turn down Warlands Lane leads to the Wyndham Cottle Almshouses. This pair of semi-detached brick and pebbledash bungalows was built in 1922, funded by a legacy left by Dr. Wyndham Cottle, who lived in the manor house. Residents of the almshouses had to be deserving married couples over the age of 65 years, but no single women.

There is an attractive walk along a bridleway south from Warlands Lane.

NITON (I)

Highly recommended for a visit, Niton contains most of the components that go to make an ideal village: church, school, public library, pub, several shops and some most attractive cottages. The village is in two parts, with the main part being a little inland from Lower Niton (or Niton Undercliff) down by the shore. They are linked by Barrack Shute.

First stop is the Church of St John the Baptist, which is mainly 13th century with some Victorian restoration. The ancient oak door opens on an interior that is unusually dark owing to the small windows, surrounding trees and dark woodwork. In the yard is the grave of Edward Edwards, the pioneer of free municipal libraries, who died in the village in 1886.

Near the church gate is an attractive, thatched stone cottage called Herveys, built in the late 17th or early 18th century. It was the home of the Willis family, who used to keep a shop there. In front of the churchyard and cottage is a pavement leading to the crossroads. Under the pavement is the River Yar, whose source is at the farm to the west of the church.

On the right towards the crossroads is the former village school, now a youth club and in Newport Road is the Methodist Chapel of 1864. On returning to the crossroads, turn left into Chatfield Road, where the Roman Catholic Church of St Joseph opened in 1969 in a former barn on the right. Farther along on the same side is the old rectory, a large late 18th century building erected on the site of an earlier rectory. Charles II was said to have spent two nights there in 1675. Opposite are some examples of Niton's picturesque stone cottages.

Returning to the centre of the village, and turning left at the crossroads, the village hall is on the left hand side of the High Street. Built as a malt house in the early 18th century, it has served many purposes in its long life, including a meeting house, school, Baptist Chapel and working men's club before finally becoming a village hall in 1936. Further along the street at the foot of Institute Hill is the old telephone exchange, which now houses the public library. The hill leads past the present village school on the left and the Baptist Chapel on the right to Niton Undercliff, from where paths lead down to the

Niton, St Catherine's Lighthouse. The 15 million candle-power light has a range of 17 miles. The farm in the foreground, Knowles Farm, was the scene of Marconi's early trials in wireless in 1900.

The engraving on the left shows the original 1838 lighthouse, before the tower was shortened to its present height of 86 feet.

much closer to sea level, and the light was first lit two years later. Later, the tower was shortened to its current 86 feet, and the flash of the light can be seen for about 17 miles. During the Second World War the lighthouse was bombed and three of the keepers were killed.

On the left of the path from Niton Undercliff down to Puckaster Cove is Puckaster Cottage of about 1813, an ornate stone-built cottage with a bowed front and a thatched roof. A classic cottage *orné* set in lovely grounds. At the bottom of the path is Puckaster Cove where in 1675 Charles II was driven ashore in a violent storm. He later went overland to Yarmouth to enjoy the hospitality of his old friend Sir Robert Holmes, Governor of the Isle of Wight.

shore. A popular stopping place is the Buddle Inn, formerly a farm.

Nearby is a lane which goes down to St Catherine's Point; the southernmost point of the Island. On a summer's day it is a lovely spot to relax and watch the yachts rounding the Point. Also here is St Catherine's Lighthouse, built to replace an earlier one that stood on the down above but which was often shrouded in fog. Work on the new lighthouse started in 1838 on a site

Niton. Puckaster Cottage, built 1812-14. A good example of a fashionable holiday home.

There are a number of walks in the area; up on the downs above the village or along the coastal path. A particularly good walk is along the old road to Blackgang. A large cliff fall in 1928

blocked the road about half a mile along and it now ends in a car park. There is, however, plenty to see, especially in the spring when the cowslips are out.

NORTHWOOD (B)

Clinging to the southern fringes of Gurnard and Cowes, Northwood appears, from the main road, to consist of little more than red-brick houses, a trading estate, a factory and a petrol station. To find the original Northwood, take the lane that leads from the main road to the west bank of the Medina. Here you will discover the Church of St John the Baptist, some ancient farm buildings, now converted into houses, and some old cottages.

The church is 12th century but the present tower and spire are 19th century. There is a fine Norman south doorway carved with chevrons, and inside is the original Norman font, which was found in the churchyard in 1954. On the east side of the main road, towards Newport, is the permanent home of the Isle of Wight County Show, an annual event that dates back to 1882. For two days in July the show brings together all aspects of country life on the Island, including the showing and judging of a wide range of animals and all manner of crafts. Next to the show ground is the Military History Museum, complete with tanks, artillery, a D-Day diorama, gift shop and café.

Norton Green.

NORTON (D)

Lies to the west of Yarmouth Harbour and in the 19th century consisted of a few stone cottages and the then recently built houses of the gentry. Today some of these large villas have been extended and converted into holiday villages with chalets in the grounds.

A short walk west along the coast at Sconce Point is Fort Victoria Country Park, whose fort was originally intended as part of the Victorian defences of the western Solent. The fort was built in 1852-53 on the site of a Napoleonic fort known as Sconce Point Battery, and was first garrisoned by a detachment of the volunteer Isle of Wight Artillery Militia. Its position and design were unsatisfactory from the outset. It was at sea-level, passing ships could see the interior, and its defences were no match for the newest Ironclad warships armed with powerful breech-loading guns firing high explosive shells. In 1876 it was recommended that the fort be demolished, but instead it was taken out of front line service and used as a barracks. Later it was used for mine-laying experiments and testing searchlights. During the Second World War the fort housed the 72nd Coastal Regiment of the Royal Artillery, who taught coastal gunnery crews. Although much of the fort has been destroyed, enough remains to make a visit rewarding. It is open to the public in the summer, and its attractions include a marine aquarium, a planetarium and a model railway. There are also some splendid views across the water to

Norton. Fort Victoria before much of it was demolished in 1969. What remains is now part of Fort Victoria Country Park.

Hurst Castle and Lymington.

To the south is the small community of Norton Green, which once had a chapel and a pub, both now converted into houses. On the high ground towards Freshwater is Golden Hill Fort, built in the 19th century as a barracks and supply depot for the fort at the west end of the Island.

The riverside walk southwards from Norton Spit to Freshwater Church is recommended.

PARKHURST (E)

A suburb of Newport on the road to Cowes, Parkhurst is known nationally for its three prisons and by locals for the Forest and as the site of the Island's hospital.

Parkhurst Forest was once the largest on the Island, extending from the west bank of the River Medina to Newtown estuary. Thickly wooded, mostly with oak with hazel underwood, one commentator writing about the forest observed that 'in the time of King Charles II . . . a squirrel might have run on the tops of trees from Gurnard to Carisbrooke'. Much of it was an unenclosed hunting ground, but Great Park and Park Place Farm at Upper Watchingwell recall the 'King's Park', a true deer park on the south-west rim of the Forest. The Forest was nominally held by the Governor of the Island, but

A clearing in Parkhurst Forest.

ABOVE RIGHT *Parkhurst. In the grounds of St Mary's Hospital is the old workhouse.*

it was really a common for the locals. Much of the ancient oak was felled to build the navy's 'wooden walls' during the Napoleonic wars. Large tracts became heathland and it was disafforested in 1812. The commons were enclosed and brought into cultivation, and new plantations were created. Today, the Forest is under the control of Forest Enterprises, who have produced a helpful trail leaflet to assist walkers enjoy some fine woodland walks.

The Island's trio of prisons owe their existence to Albany Barracks, built during the Napoleonic Wars and condemned by Keats as 'a nest of debauchery'. Parkhurst's first prison opened as Parkhurst Juvenile Reformatory in 1838 on the site of the barracks hospital; indeed, an original building still stands within the prison walls. Here juvenile offenders were trained in skills such as cobbling and blacksmithing before being transported to Australia. Later, for a short time, it held women prisoners, but in 1869 they were replaced with men. In the 1970s Parkhurst became a maximum security prison, but after several escapes and a government report, it became a

Category 'B' prison. A second prison, Camp Hill, was opened in 1911. Parkhurst's inmates helped build it, first clearing an area of forest and then making the building blocks on the site. For many years Camp Hill was a Preventative Detention Prison, but in 1931 it was required as a Borstal Institution, and the men were removed to other prisons. Today it is a Closed Category 'C' prison. In 1967 Albany Prison was opened as a medium security

prison on the site of the old barracks.

Of greater importance to the health and welfare of most Islanders is St Mary's Hospital, which opened in 1991 at a cost of some £30 million. A fine example of contemporary architecture, it pioneered the use of low-energy materials to control heat loss. The hospital is set in landscaped grounds whose attractive lake is home to large numbers of ducks.

In the hospital grounds is the Island

Parkhurst Prison. A Victorian engraving of the prison. The building on the extreme left was the prison lunatic asylum.

Parkurst Prison. The white house on the right is one of the original prison buildings, and once was the Governor's House.

workhouse, erected in the 1770s as the House of Industry. The brick building was, in its time, one of the largest and most expensive workhouses in England, with accommodation for 600 paupers – men, women and children. It remained open until the 1940s, and the building is still used by the hospital.

PORCHFIELD (E)

This small and peaceful village is best approached from the main Newport to Yarmouth road by the turn into Whitehouse Road.

In Colemans Lane is the popular Colemans Animal Farm, once a working dairy farm and now offering visitors hands-on experience of life on a farm.

A row of houses leads into the centre of the village, through which the wonderfully named Rodge Brook runs north into Clamerkin Lake (which isn't a lake at all, but a tidal finger of Newton River).

One house in the approach into the village is a former Bible Christian Chapel, first erected in 1852. Until the opening of the chapel, in what was then called Dirty Lane, services had been held first in the open air and then in local cottages. At the road junction is the village centre with its pub and village hall while a short distance along the road to Cowes, on the right, is the site of the Bethel Chapel of 1835. Although the building has now gone, the adjoining cemetery remains and is still in use.

In the west of the village is the hamlet

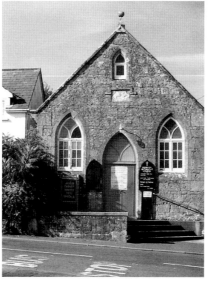

Rookley. Three views of the village.

of Lock's Green. The imposing building on the right was built, in 1870, as the church and school, but is now a private house. Close by is Jersey Camp, a military firing range that covers a large coastal area to the north of Porchfield. As the surrounding countryside is flat and largely free of traffic, there are several good walks, particularly along Elmsworth Lane to the seashore. The range is still in use so it is important to look out for the red warning flags when planning walks.

ROOKLEY (F)

A small village, close to the geographical centre of the Island,

which, until its expansion in the last century, was focused on the junction of the roads from Godshill and Niton. Here is the Green, which was laid out to mark the Queen's Silver Jubilee in 1977 and has recently been enlarged, and is an ideal place to sit to study the village map or enjoy a picnic.

Close to the Green is the former Bible Christian Chapel of 1859, and still a place of worship. On the main road opposite the Green is the former school building, which became a private house and had a porch added in 1959. Farther along the road, to the left, is an industrial estate built on the site of what was once one of the largest brickworks on the Island. It was the last still to

Porchfield. The village crossroads.

operate on the Island when it finally closed in 1978. Afterwards, the old clay pits were landscaped and became Rookley Country Park, which now consists of a pub, caravan park, lakes and children's amusements.

There is an enjoyable walk to the west of the village. Head towards Loverstone Farm and turn south and return via Rookley Farm.

ROUD (I)

A group of four farms and a few cottages lying to the west of the Godshill to Whitwell road. Little traffic passes this way and, indeed, it is a difficult place to find. Nearby is Beacon Alley, which, as its name suggests, is a narrow, steep-sided lane which once lead to the invasion warning beacon on Bleak Down.

RYDE (C)

For visitors arriving by catamaran from Portsmouth or by hovercraft from Southsea, the first view of the Island is of the historic seaside town of Ryde. Much of what they see today is a Regency planned town and still contains a rich legacy of early 19th century buildings.

Before the town was laid out, it

comprised two separate communities: Lower Ryde, by the shore, which consisted of a row of cottages and two or three inns and where small scale shipbuilding was carried out, and Upper Ryde (where the High Street stands today), where farms lined both sides of the road. The farmers worked the surrounding fields, which were, like 95 per cent of the land in the area, owned by the lord of the manor.

This large-scale land ownership gave the lord of the manor a great deal of influence in the development of Ryde. In the late 18th century the incumbent lord, William Player, decided to lay out a gridiron pattern of streets between Lower and Upper Ryde, thus creating the modern town. He began by building

Ryde. An early 19th century engraving of the village green in what was then Upper Ryde. Behind the trees on the left is the first St Thomas's Chapel.

a new wide street to link the two communities. Started in about 1790, it was first named Middle Ryde, but later renamed Union Street after the Union of England and Ireland in 1801. From this first phase grew the pattern of streets which today form the eastern nucleus of the town, including Cross, George, Melville and Castle Streets. To carry on this development after William's death

Ryde. An 1836 engraving of the pier. In the centre is Brigstocke Terrace which, like many of the buildings shown, still stands.

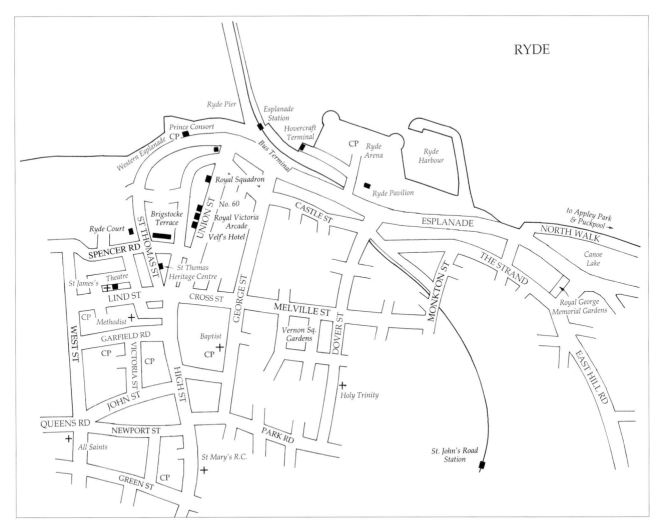

Ryde Pier
Esplanade Station
Prince Consort
CP
Hovercraft Terminal
Western Esplanade
Bus Terminal
CP
Ryde Arena
Ryde Harbour
Royal Squadron
Ryde Pavilion
No. 60
Royal Victoria Arcade
CASTLE ST
ESPLANADE
to Appley Park & Puckpool
Brigstocke Terrace
ST THOMAS ST
UNION ST
Velf's Hotel
NORTH WALK
Ryde Court
SPENCER RD
GEORGE ST
Canoe Lake
St Thomas Heritage Centre
THE STRAND
MONKTON ST
St James's
Theatre
LIND ST
CROSS ST
MELVILLE ST
Royal George Memorial Gardens
CP
Methodist
DOVER ST
WEST ST
GARFIELD RD
Baptist
Vernon Sq. Gardens
EAST HILL RD
CP
VICTORIA ST
CP
CP
HIGH ST
JOHN ST
Holy Trinity
QUEENS RD
NEWPORT ST
PARK RD
All Saints
St Mary's R.C.
St. John's Road Station
GREEN ST
CP

in 1792, his widow, Jane, obtained a private Act of Parliament allowing her to grant 99 year building leases. It proved a far-sighted move. The increasing popularity of sea bathing with the wealthy and improving transport links between the Island and mainland meant that building plots were quickly snapped up and the town grew rapidly.

Some of the fine villas built by the wealthy still stand. Westmont, on Queen's Road, is now part of Ryde School, but was originally built in 1819 by Jane Player's daughter, Elizabeth, and her husband Dr John Lind: Lind Street recalls his contribution to Ryde's

Ryde, Queen's Road. Westmont was built in 1819 for John Lind, ground landlord of half of Ryde, and is now part of Ryde School.

Ryde. The view over the town from the tower of All Saints Church. Brigstocke Terrace is to the right and behind is the Pier.

development. The tall tower of the house originally built by the 2nd Earl Spencer, Westfield House, still dominates Westfield Park. Buckingham Villa, west of Union Street, is now flats, but dates to 1813 and was once the seaside home of the Marquess of Buckingham.

A key factor in the growth of the town was the construction of the pier in 1813-14. Prior to the pier people and goods were landed from wherries on the open beach and transferred to dry land by horse and cart, an unpopular undignified procedure dependent on the state of the tide. Many visitors chose to disembark at Cowes and journey to Ryde by road. In 1812 the local gentry obtained the necessary Act of Parliament to build a pier out to the low-water mark.

Ryde Pier is the oldest in England and, at 703 metres (2305 feet), the fourth longest. In 1862-64 a tramway pier was constructed on the east side of the existing structure and in 1879-80 a railway pier was built next to the now dismantled tramway. The Island Line railway carries electric trains from the pier head to Shanklin, and from the pier head there is a fast Wightlink catamaran service to Portsmouth Harbour. The hovercraft service to Southsea – which takes just ten minutes – leaves from the

shore next to the pier entrance.

The splendid Esplanade, which runs from the bottom of Union Street to Appley, did not exist 200 years ago. The cottages of Lower Ryde (where the amusement arcades now stand) were then on the beach. Since the early 19th century the town has been expanding out to sea and the more recently reclaimed areas are where the ice rink and Harbour can now be found.

A walk along the Esplanade is strongly recommended. As well as the beach and fine views across the Solent, Ryde has a range of entertainment for all ages, including the Canoe Lake and Appley Park. At the far end is the castellated Appley Tower, a folly of about 1870. A plaque on the sea wall commemorates the 780 convicts of the First Fleet, which anchored offshore before setting sail for Australia's Botany Bay in 1787.

One of the oldest buildings on the seaward side of the Esplanade is the former Ryde Pavilion, built in 1926-27

Ryde. Appley Tower, a folly of about 1870.

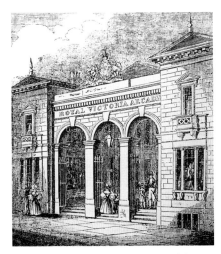

Ryde. Royal Victoria Arcade; one of the oldest shopping arcades in England.

Ryde, Lind Street. The Colonnade was built late in the 1830s and behind is the former Town Hall of 1829-31.

and now the entrance to the LA Bowl (*see colour section*). A recent addition is the Royal George Memorial Garden at the junction of the Strand and East Hill Road, laid out in 2004 as a memorial to the 800 lives lost when the *Royal George* sank in the Solent in 1782.

Near the Western Esplanade, in St Thomas's Street, is the imposing Prince Consort building. Built as the clubhouse for the Royal Victoria Yacht Club, the foundation stone was laid in 1846 by Prince Albert. In 1965 the club moved to Fishbourne and the building was sold and subsequently renamed.

Union Street remains Ryde's principal thoroughfare, with fine seaward views. Buildings of interest include the Royal

RIGHT *Ryde, looking south up Union Street.*

BELOW *Ryde. Statues depicting the seasons on the parapet above No. 60 Union Street.*

Squadron, which opened as an hotel in 1835 and was used by Queen Victoria while she arranged the purchase of Osborne House. Further up the hill is No 60, distinguished by the four statues on its parapet, which are said to represent the seasons. This was the home and business headquarters of Hughes and Mullins, the famous 19th century royal court photographers. A few doors further up is the imposing Italian style frontage of the Royal Victoria Arcade of 1835-36, one of the first shopping arcades in England. Further still is Yelf's Hotel, which dates

back to 1801-02 and was the first hotel in Ryde.

At the top of the street is St Thomas's Square, originally the village green. Leading off the Square is Lind Street and Ryde Theatre, which boasts a fine clock tower. Built in 1829-31 as the Town Hall it became the largest such building on the Island and still houses council offices as well as the theatre. Close by in St Thomas's Street is the former church of St Thomas's. One of the oldest buildings in Ryde, it was erected in 1827 on the site of an earlier chapel. There is an attractive rest garden

next door. The building has been fully restored, and is open to the public. Inside are the pew of the Lord of The Manor and several memorials to former lords and other Ryde notables. Some of the original box pews remain, one with its own heater.

Further down St Thomas's Street is Brigstocke Terrace, a fine Regency terrace of 10 houses built 1826-29 to the designs of the London architect, James Sanderson (who also designed Ryde Town Hall and St Thomas's Church). They were often leased out to wealthy visitors, and are now a block of apartments, some with lovely views of the Solent. Across the road is a smaller terrace of four houses, Ryde Court, erected in 1853, and taken together they give some idea of the wealth of Ryde's 19th century visitors.

The narrow High Street is the oldest part of the town and contains a wide range of small buildings of various ages. It was along this street that sheep fattened on the downs to the south of Ryde would have been driven en route to the shore and, from there, to the mainland for sale. Also in the High Street is St Mary's Roman Catholic Church of 1846, designed by Joseph Hansom, more celebrated as the designer of the Hansom cab.

In Garfield Road is the stone-built Methodist Church (1883) while the Baptist Church, in George Street, is brick-built and dates from 1862.

Ryde has three Church of England churches, the oldest of which is St James's in Lind Street, which dates from 1827. The next is Holy Trinity, in Dover Street, which has a distinctive tower and spire and was built in 1845 but has later additions. The jewel in the crown – and perhaps the finest church on the Island – is All Saints in Queen's Road. Designed by the distinguished architect George Gilbert Scott it was built in three phases between 1869 and 1891. The 180 feet steeple is a fine sight, specially when floodlit at night. The west door gives entrance to a long wide nave of six bays with slender piers. The font was also designed by Scott and

Ryde. All Saints Church, whose 180 feet high spire is one of the town's landmarks.

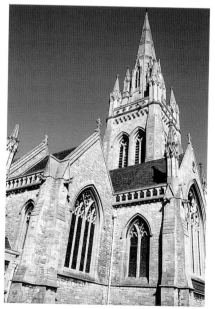

commemorates the Prince of Wales' (later Edward VII) recovery from a serious illness. The pulpit is of Derbyshire alabaster. The high alter is of olive wood from the Holy Land and was carved in Jerusalem.

There are a number of fine walks in and around Ryde, one of the most popular of which is along the Esplanade, through Appley Park to Puckpool. This can be extended through Springvale to the village of Seaview. Another excellent route is through Spencer Road and on to Ladies Walk, through the golf course to Binstead Church. This can be extended to take in the considerable attractions of Quarr Abbey. Those favouring a countryside walk should take the footpath at the western end of Playstreet Lane (south west of Ryde) and continue beyond the Millennium Green, which is worth exploring, and on to Dame Anthony's Common. There are several paths to take from the Common, including one that leads to Havenstreet.

Today Ryde, which stretches from Binstead in the west to Elmfield and Oakfield in the east, and inland to Haylands and Swanmore, has a lot to offer, both to the visitor and resident. There are safe sandy beaches, and ready-made amusements offering something of interest for both the youngest and oldest. History and architecture combine neatly in the town centre and adjoining streets. Melville Street, with its beautiful Vernon Square Gardens, Queen's Road and Spencer Road give a good flavour of Regency Ryde.

A more unusual outing is by rail, on an electric underground train which travels overground. The Island Line operates these former London tube trains from Ryde Pier Head to Shanklin, with stops at Ryde Esplanade, Ryde St John's, Brading, Sandown and Lake. During the summer the trains also call at Smallbrook Interchange to connect with the Isle of Wight Railway steam trains to Havenstreet and Wootton.

Defence

Throughout its long history the Isle of Wight has been vulnerable because of its strategic position, and as a consequence has been invaded or threatened on many occasions. Whoever holds the Island controls an important stretch of the English south coast, including the Solent and the ports of Southampton and Portsmouth. Among the early invaders of the Island were the Romans, who arrived in the 1st century.

Today we can gain some insight as to how the Romans lived on the Island by visiting the Newport and Brading Roman villas. The Newport villa has a particularly interesting bath range and at Brading there are some of the finest mosaics in England.

The fall of the Roman Empire in the 5th century and the associated withdrawal of the Roman army left the Island open to invasion once again, this time by the pagan Jutes. The Christian Saxons had taken control by the 7th century but during this period the Island was raided several times by the Vikings who sometimes made it their winter base.

Further changes came with the Normans after 1066. They built a castle at Carisbrooke, near Newport, and made it the administrative head-quarters of the Island. William the Conqueror gave

Carisbrooke Castle gatehouse.

the Island to William Fitz Osbern. In 1100 it passed to Richard de Redvers and it was his son Baldwin who replaced the initial timber defences of the castle with the stone-built curtain wall. The last of the family was the remarkable Countess Isabella de Fortibus, a widow at 26, Lady of the Wight, and one of the wealthiest women in the country. She made the Castle her principal residence, converting the interior into domestic quarters suitable for a lady of her station. On her deathbed she sold the Lordship of the Island and her property to Edward I.

Because of its strategic importance Carisbrooke Castle has remained crown land ever since. Lords of

Carisbrooke Castle.

Fort Albert was built in the 19th century to protect the entrance to the western Solent.

A Second World War gun emplacement on Culver Down. The original battery dates to the beginning of the 20th century.

the Island were appointed to govern the Island on the crown's behalf, each in his turn making alterations and additions. Its need was proven when French forces raided the Island several times in the 14th century. In 1377 the French landed and laid siege to the Castle, and according to a 16th century historian the siege was lifted when a local archer killed the French commander. Around the Island coast a watch was kept and in some places bulwarks were set up. For example there is a record of one at Ryde with a single gun mounted. It is thought that there was another at Gurnard.

Henry VIII was the next monarch to improve the defences of the Island. He had small castles or forts built at Yarmouth, to cover the entrance to the western Solent, at West and East Cowes to defend the entrance to the River Medina, and at Sandown to cover the open beach of Sandown Bay. The bulwark at Ryde was also repaired and improved. Today only the castle at Yarmouth and remnants of the Cowes castle remain.

The reign of Elizabeth I brought the threat of invasion from the Spanish. The Queen sent her cousin Sir George Cary to inspect the Island's defences. He ordered the walls of Carisbrooke Castle to be repaired and constructed two towers to mount cannons. The most significant alteration was the building of new outer defences. However, the Spanish showed no interest in the Island, and the armada fleet sailed further up the Channel to its eventual destruction.

During the Napoleonic Wars a barracks was built near Newport. Two large water mills on the River Medina were commandeered to house troops waiting to board ships in the Solent to take them to mainland Europe.

The mid-19th century saw another French invasion scare, and huge amounts of money were spent (and largely wasted) on new fortifications to guard the Solent and Portsmouth. The entrance to the western Solent was further protected by the erection of brick-built forts, Forts Albert and Victoria. More were built at the eastern end of the Island, at Sandown and on Bembridge Down. In addition four new forts were built out to sea on shoals between the Island and Portsmouth – on Spit Bank, No Man's Land, Horse Sand, and off St Helen's.

At the beginning of the 20th century Culver Battery, on Bembridge Down, was completed and shortly before the Second World War Bouldnor Battery, near Yarmouth, was built and armed.

During both World Wars the forts and batteries were manned. In the Second World War there were 9.2 inch guns at the New Needles Battery, whilst the Old Needles Battery was used by the Royal Navy to control all ship movements through the Needles Passage.

Today some of the fortifications are open to the public, though many have been engulfed by housing and holiday camps. The most interesting is Carisbrooke Castle with its long history and associations with Charles I. The whole family can enjoy a day there exploring the castle walls and rooms and the spectacular views across the Island from the castle keep. There is a museum explaining the history of the castle. Popular with adults and children alike is the well house, where a donkey in a

The Black Arrow space rocket being tested on High Down.

wheel raises a bucket of water from the deep well.

Yarmouth Castle is open to the public during the summer months and has excellent views across the western Solent. The fort at Sandown is now the home of the Isle of Wight Zoo and is open to the public. The Old Needles Battery is now owned by the National Trust and is open to the public in the summer. The New Needles Battery was used as a testing site between 1956 and 1971 for the Saunders-Roe Black Arrow space research rocket project, but is now deserted. Fort Victoria, between Yarmouth and Freshwater, is the only 19th century fort open to the public, but much of it has been demolished.

The Old Needles Battery, with two of the restored guns in place.

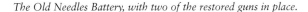

ST HELENS (G)

A village green that is said to be the largest in England lies at the heart of the village of St Helens, on the western side of Bembridge Harbour. The Green, surrounded by houses, stone-built cottages and shops, provides a lovely setting and is the hub of village life. There is a children's play area, football and cricket pitches and seats.

On Upper Green Road is 'Freefolk', the cottage where Sophie Dawes, daughter of a local smuggler, was born in about 1792. Later known as the Queen of Chantilly, she ran away to London, became the mistress of the Duc de Bourbon (whose murder she later plotted) and went on to live a life of considerable luxury in Paris, even marrying a French nobleman. She died in 1840, her looks faded, but the church-

St Helens. The infamous Sophie Daws, daughter of a smuggler.

yard contains her magnificent memorial to her nephew James Dawes (who she also may have poisoned). Nearby is 'Little Shell House', whose end is covered in local seashells depicting Island scenes. Bobby Allen, the village electrician, started to cover his house with shells in the 1950's, and the various scenes were designed by a local artist, Willy Wright. On the same road is the Vine Inn and, next door, the building that used to be the village pub with its name, 'Sailors' Home', still visible at the front of the building. At the north end of the Green is St Helens Community Centre and adjoining it is St Catherine's Chapel, conveniently placed for those unable to travel to the parish church, which is between the village and Nettlestone.

At the bottom of the Duver (dialect for sandy piece of waste ground) Road, by the shore, are the remains of the former Church of St Helen's. The tower is all that remains of the Cluniac Priory founded in the 11th century and suppressed by Edward IV, who bestowed it on Eton College. Little was done to maintain the church and by the mid 16th century salt winds, erosion and neglect had left much of it in ruins, but the tower remains a famous sea-mark. In 1719 a new church was built inland on the road to Nettlestone. It was mostly rebuilt in 1831 and the chancel added later.

Until Georgian times the village was small and centred around the Green. It grew by victualling shipping anchored offshore in St Helen's Roads with fresh food and drinking water (the local water was said to have good keeping qualities). The priory ruins reputedly were the source of a soft sandstone – Holy Stone, or holystone – used for scouring ship's decks. Another substantial income derived from smuggling, with several villagers

St Helens, Upper Green Road. To the right of the telegraph pole and on the front of the brick house is a plaque marking the birthplace of Sophie Daws.

St Helens. The tower is all that is left of the old church and is now a seamark.

involved. At the bottom of Station Road, on the way to Bembridge, is the old railway station, now a private house.

The Duver consists of sand dunes to the north of the village. On the north side is the sea wall with a quaint row of former railway carriages serving as beach huts. At the eastern end of the shore are the commercial activities, including boat yards. The area inland from the sand dunes was once the home of the Royal Isle of Wight Golf Links, which opened in 1882 and whose small clubhouse still stands. The whole area was gifted to the National Trust in 1961 and is open to the public and can be explored on foot.

Another interesting walk is down Mill Road to the edge of the Harbour. Turn left around Mill House and along the bank across the pond to the Duver. There are fine views across the Harbour towards Bembridge.

Prominent offshore is St Helen's Fort, started in 1867 to guard the anchorage, and used as a gun emplacement in both World Wars.

ST LAWRENCE (I)

The village is to the west of Ventnor, on a plateau between the shore cliff and the inner cliff. It stretches along both sides of the Undercliff Drive – the road from Ventnor to Niton – and because it is sheltered from the north it traditionally enjoys a mild climate.

There are two churches, the more recent of which is a real highlight for enthusiasts of Victorian architecture. The Church of St Lawrence, in Undercliff Drive, was designed by Sir George Gilbert Scott and opened in 1878. The church's glory is its magnificent Pre-Raphaelite stained glass by William Morris, Ford Madox-Brown and Sir Edward Burne-Jones. Ford Madox-Brown's design showing St Luke the physician holding a copy of Hippocrates tells us something about the windows' origins. They were originally installed in the chapel of the Royal National Hospital (*see* Ventnor),

St Lawrence. In the new church is some fine stained glass by William Morris. This window depicts the raising of Jairus's daughter.

The 'new' Church of St Lawrence.

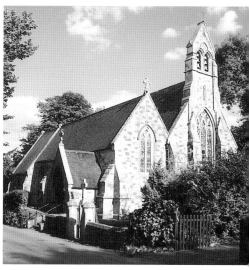

which stood on the site of the Ventnor Botanic Garden car park and was demolished in 1969.

The Old Church of St Lawrence is in Seven Sisters Road, a small, low building with a bellcote (whose bell came from Appuldurcombe). It is known to have existed in 1200, probably as a chapel for the lord of the manor. Until 1842, when a chancel was

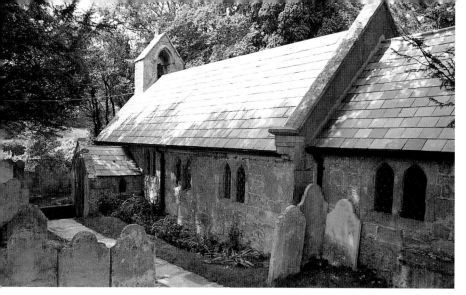

ABOVE *St Lawrence. The old church was at one time the smallest complete parish church in England.*

RIGHT *St Lawrence. An Arts and Crafts cottage in Seven Sisters Road of 1937.*

added, it was the smallest complete parish church in England, measuring approximately 25ft x 11ft. The inside was lit by oil lamps and candles until electricity was installed in 1970. The royal arms are of Charles I and also of note are the Georgian hat pegs.

At the west end of Seven Sisters Road are three attractive cottages with rendered walls and thatched roofs. They were designed by the well known Arts and Crafts architect, Baillie Scott

(*see also* Bembridge), and built in 1937.

The area contains some fine large houses, including Old Park, formerly the home of William Spindler, a German millionaire who planned a model village around the house, but only got as far as

building some sea defences, whose remains can still be seen on the beach at Binnel Point (*see also* Undercliff). Today the house is an hotel, in whose grounds some converted farm buildings are home to Isle of Wight Glass, founded in 1973 by the glassmaker Michael Harris. You can watch glass-blowers at work, and their beautifully crafted hand-blown studio glass is for sale in the showroom.

From the coastal path you have views of Lisle Combe, a large, brick house with wonderful decorative barge-boards and a profusion of oriel windows that was the home of the poet Alfred Noyes (1880-1958), and is still lived in by his descendents (*see* 'Writers and Poets').

The centre of St Lawrence has two other buildings of interest. Craigie Lodge was the home of Pearl Mary Craigie (1867-1906), a now largely forgotten novelist who wrote under the name of John Oliver Hobbes. A short distance along the road towards Niton, on the left, opposite the junction with Seven Sisters Road, is the Old Toll House. Built in 1852, it collected road tolls until the abolition of the turnpikes in 1889.

A walk along the top of the inner cliff offers views down on the village and out across the English Channel. A second good walk is along St Rhadegund's path, north to Whitwell.

St Lawrence The old toll house beside the main road.

St Lawrence, Old Park, now a hotel but formerly the Victorian home of the German millionaire, William Spindler.

Local Building Tradition

MARION BRINTON

The distinctive character of an area or region is made up as much by the traditional buildings as by the landscape. If, for example, one was to envisage the typical scene of the Cotswolds or Peak District, buildings undoubtedly feature. This is no accident; buildings and landscape are necessarily related by the underlying geology.

Local building traditions, or 'vernacular architecture', are influenced primarily by the availability of suitable building materials. Before the advent of cheap transportation brought about by the arrival of the railways, builders sought their materials close at hand, perhaps as near as the next field or local coppice. Without doubt those constructing vernacular buildings (which generally includes farmhouses, cottages and farm buildings) on the Isle of Wight would have sourced the materials on the Island. Those with higher aspirations and designing in a more 'polite' style, for perhaps a public building such as a church or a town hall, or maybe a small country house, would have imported some of the materials, for example Portland stone. For these buildings the attention to architectural style and detail was important, as was the desire to demonstrate your wealth. No such luxury for the vernacular builder.

The building materials used not only affected the colour and texture of the building but also influenced the design and detailing. Thus the most durable building stone would be put to good use in supporting the corners of the building, or forming the protective mouldings and copings where exposure to the weather was at is most destructive. As knowledge was passed down an intimate understanding of materials developed, insuring the best use of what was available or affordable. The buildings were constructed by 'amateurs', quite possibly for their own use, perhaps assisted by a stone mason. Hence a discernable local building tradition developed particular to a said area. At times the changes are subtle, perhaps the pitch of a roof or the style of dormer windows, especially at the edge of regions where one tradition melds into another. But on the Island the insularity defined the tradition quite naturally. The traditional building style of the Island lacks a uniformity which you might otherwise expect. This was a result of the Island being blessed with a variety of building materials including stone, timber and brick.

The vernacular buildings which have survived are largely those constructed from the late 16th and early 17th century through to the middle part of the 19th century. They are also the most durable of those built. The farm labourer's humble dwelling was usually built of timber, earth and thatch. Once

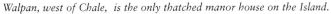

Walpan, west of Chale, is the only thatched manor house on the Island.

it ceased to be serviceable it was either abandoned or replaced. The cottages, farmhouses and small manor houses which have survived were the homes of those who could afford to use stone, brick (rarely) and on occasion substantial timber framing.

The vernacular period ends with the expansion of the canal and railway network, resulting in the spread of not only materials, such as Welsh slate, but also the dissemination of ideas of style. By the latter part of the Victorian period buildings were being constructed on the Island which were no longer firmly rooted in the vernacular tradition. The roof was likely to be slated and the style probably more influenced by the Italian villa than the Island farmhouse.

The Isle of Wight is fortunate in that it has ample building stone readily available. However, stone was not used extensively in domestic buildings until the 17th century, and it is perhaps the stone manor houses, farmhouses and cottages of the 1600's which are the most distinctive on the Island. Many examples survive today, particularly in the southern half of the Island. It was not until the development of the Island brickworks in the 19th century that the predominance of stone as the most popular building material was challenged.

All the building stone on the Island is sedimentary in origin, meaning that although it was relatively easily quarried, cut and carved it was not especially durable compared to other stone. Geologically the oldest of the building stones is the sandstone from the Wealden Group. Sandstone has a high iron content, giving it a characteristic orange or golden brown colour. The stone comes to the surface in a relatively confined area on the south west coast, and can be widely seen in Brook, Shorwell and Brighstone. A good example is a stone wall surrounding Grange Farm at Brighstone, where the stone was probably brought up the chine from the beach below.

A similar building stone is extracted from the Lower Greensand deposits which outcrop in the Shorwell, Brighstone and Mottistone area. Several of the cottages in Shorwell are of a lovely mellow orange-brown and one wing of Wolverton Manor in Shorwell is constructed of the sandstone.

The Upper Greensand series yields a quite different building stone. These rocks follow the central chalk ridge and form a narrow band across the Island which broadens out in the Gatcombe and Chillerton area. These sandstones also form the bedrock of the area to the north of the southern chalk ridge around Niton, Whitwell and Wroxall. This stone is grey-green in colour and weathers rapidly. It is usually seen used as rubble (rough, un-squared blocks) and is rarely found in large blocks. Nevertheless its use was widespread, particularly in the south, and was even exported to be used in the construction of Winchester and Chichester cathedrals. It was also employed on the Island for the grander buildings, such as Appuldurcombe House at Wroxall and Gatcombe House, Gatcombe.

Chalk is an easily recognised building material. Although it was extensively quarried to make lime mortar, plasters and for the rubble core to walls it was less common as a facing stone. Chalk is extremely soft and porous, and therefore susceptible to weathering. It was a walling material of last resort, only used where better stones were either unavailable or unaffordable, and wherever possible in conjunction with either brick or stone for the more vulnerable areas. The chalk blocks were cut very precisely, making their surface smooth and flat, thus minimising the crevices for water to penetrate. Chalk was most common in the Brighstone and Mottistone area, but also in Arreton and Havenstreet.

The youngest of the Island building stones are the Bembridge Limestones, which are a mere 35 million years old. They are fresh water limestones and have a high fossil content. They fall into two types: the Binstead Stone and Quarr Stone. They are similar in appearance being cream or grey in colour, but the shell fragments in Quarr Stone have a more crushed appearance. The Romans exported Quarr Stone to Fishbourne near Chichester for the construction of a villa. The stone was then quarried and exported throughout the Saxon and medieval periods for use throughout Hampshire. The Bembridge Limestone is the hardest of the local stones but because the quarries on the north coast had largely been exhausted by the medieval period its survival is rarer. Fullingmills Farmhouse near Calbourne is an

ABOVE LEFT *A typical Island cottage opposite Shorwell Church.*

ABOVE *Timber-framing at Brading, a Tudor town house now part of the Brading Experience.*

LEFT *A 17th century timber clad house in the centre of Brading.*

example, but otherwise it can be seen used more sparingly for plinths and quoins.

Flint, which is found in bands in the chalk, was also available in abundance. However, it was rarely used where better options were available, so is scarce on the Island. The greatest concentration of flint buildings on the Island is in the Ventnor and Bonchurch area, where there was a great deal of building in the mid 19th century as Ventnor's reputation as a seaside resort grew. Supplies of local stone were unable to meet the demand. In addition, access to Ventnor was relatively difficult because of the surrounding steep hills. Flint was locally plentiful and easy to transport. But it was also unfashionable, so its use is usually relegated to the back and sides of buildings.

Very few timber-framed buildings survive on the Island, most being demolished to make way for better stone-built dwellings. Those that remain suggest that the Island did not conform to one

particular tradition of timber construction. There are examples of box framing, common across the south and east of England; cruck framing (using paired timbers to form the main cross frames), which was more common in the west and north of England; and even one example of close studding (use of lots of vertical timbers set close together), which is more typical of East Anglia. The most impressive of the surviving timber buildings on the Island must be the close studding at Osborne Smith Wax Works (The Brading Experience) in Brading.

Brick, so common across much of England, was little used on the Island until well into the 19th century. Nettlestone Manor near Ryde is thought to be the oldest brick building, dating from the latter part of the 16th century. The earliest brick building with a datestone (1615) is Merstone Manor, near Arreton. The examples of pre-Victorian brick buildings are generally found in the north of the Island, where there was not the easy access to building stone, but where there were the sands and clays for brick-making. As Newport and Cowes expanded in the 18th century, followed by Ryde, brick-making developed on an ad hoc basis as small kilns were set up on the edge of the towns to meet the ready market. The Island brick is typically a soft

red, but its colours can range from oranges through to a red-purple.

None of the roofing materials were peculiar to the Island. Thatch was traditional, and much still remains, particularly in Brighstone and Godshill. As brick making expanded clay tiles became more readily available. Slate was used from the mid 19th century and its use quickly spread. There are a couple of examples of the use of Purbeck stone slates (Hanover House at Brook, and Mottistone Manor) for the lower courses of the roof. It would have been relatively easy to import Purbeck slates by sea direct from Swanage, so it is intriguing that Purbeck stone tiles are not more common.

The vernacular architecture of the Island is perhaps typified by its variety. However, any attempt to pick out a distinctive building type which best exemplifies the Island tradition would surely select the stone–built farmhouse of the early 17th century. A fine example of such a building is the privately owned Lower Farmhouse, Chale. It is a two bay stone house with a lobby entry (ie. with the front door in line with a central stack). At the back is an outshut, rather like a lean-to, and the rear slope of the roof drops to a low eave. The original roof must have been thatched and the walls at the gable ends were extended upwards beyond the verge to give protection to the thatch from wind damage.

The windows are metal casements with leaded lights within stone frames with stone mullions. The windows and door on the ground floor have a drip mould or hood mould over the top. As the name suggests this gave the ill-fitting windows some protection from rain water running down the face of the wall. The walls are constructed of coursed rubble and are built on a substantial stone plinth capped with coping stones.

On entering the front door there is a small lobby, on the right is one room and on the left is another. These rooms were heated by back-to-back fireplaces in the central stack. On the far side of the stack would have been a simple staircase giving access to the floor above where there were two more rooms. The history of this property has been traced back to 1613, and it is likely that it dates from around that time.

TOP *One of the few examples of the use of Purbeck stone slates is at Hanover House at Brook.*

CENTRE *Nettlestone Manor is thought to be the oldest brick building on the Island.*

BOTTOM *A recently restored stone built house at Chale.*

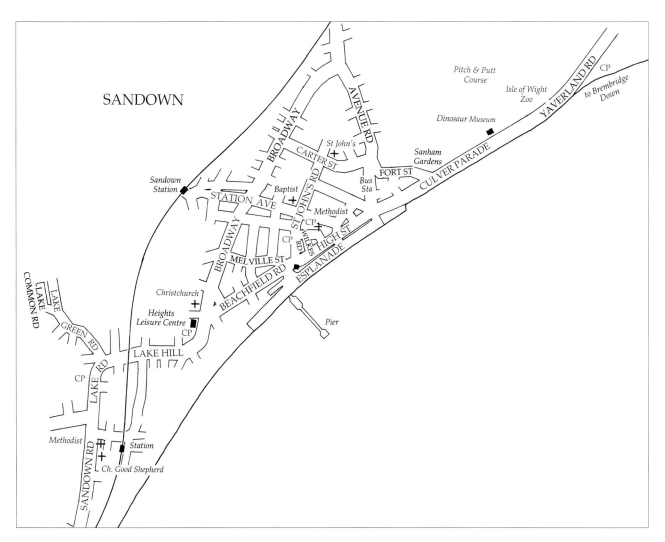

SANDOWN

Pitch & Putt Course

Isle of Wight Zoo

Dinosaur Museum

AVENUE RD

BROADWAY

CARTER ST

St John's

Sanham Gardens

FORT ST

YAVERLAND RD

CP

to Brembridge Down

CULVER PARADE

Sandown Station

Baptist

STATION AVE

Bus Sta

Methodist

BROADWAY

ST JOHN'S RD

CP

WILKES RD

HIGH ST

MELVILLE ST

CP

CP

Christchurch

BEACHFIELD RD

ESPLANADE

Heights Leisure Centre

CP

Pier

LAKE COMMON RD

GREEN RD

LAKE HILL

LAKE RD

CP

Methodist

Station

SANDOWN RD

Ch. Good Shepherd

SANDOWN (G)

With its long sandy beach and some of the Island's best-known attractions, Sandown is a renowned seaside resort that remains highly popular for family holidays (*also see colour section*).

What is now Sandown was a small group of cottages known as Sandham as late as 1800. There was a fort and some barracks, and Sandham Cottage. The cottage had been leased to John Wilkes, the radical politician in 1788, who added elaborate embellishments such as the Tuscan Room, and built tented pavilions in the gardens. Although long since demolished, there is a plaque marking the site where the house stood in Wilkes Road. Nearby, in Melville Street, is a rare Edward VIII letter box.

Sandown in summer.

Sandown from the air.

The catalyst for the major expansion of the town was the arrival of the railway from Ryde in 1864. The population grew from 1,743 in 1861 to 3,500 in 1881, and even today the town's economy remains largely dependent on its visitors. Gradually lodging houses sprung up, the mile long Esplanade was built, and new streets were laid out.

Erection of the pier started in 1876, opening three years later with a length of 360 feet. In 1895 it was extended to 875 feet and a pavilion and landing stage for paddle steamers were constructed at the pier head. Flanking the entrance of the extended pier were two elegant toll booths. In 1934 Lord Jellicoe, the famed First World War admiral who lived at St Lawrence, opened the new pavilion at the shore end. The elegant summer shows of the years between the wars are a thing of the past. Today it is a sophisticated amusement park, complete with restaurant, rides, shops and attractions.

The Isle of Wight Zoo, on Culver Parade, first opened in the late 1940s in a redundant fort and is now home to a

ABOVE *Sandown. An early 20th century photograph of longshoremen and bathing machines on the beach.*

BELOW *Sandown. Sandham Gardens with the boating lake beyond.*

LEFT *Sandown, Dinosaur Museum.*

BELOW LEFT *Sandown. A drawing of the star-shaped second fort of the 1630s, now the site of Sandham Gardens.*

Sandown Fort, Yaverland Battery and Redcliff Battery completely covered the beach. Sandown's third fort is now the home of the Isle of Wight Zoo. (*see also* Defence of the Island).

Several famous people have stayed in Sandown, including Charles Darwin (1809-1882) who began writing his *Origin of Species* (1859) whilst staying at the King's Head Hotel (now demolished). Another visitor was Lewis Carroll (1832-1898) who wrote at least part of *The Hunting of the Snark* when stayed in a lodging house on the site of the Regent Court in the High Street. (*see* Writers and Poets).

The Yaverland car park marks the beginning of a popular walk up to the top of Bembridge Down, where the views are magnificent. Another fine walk is along the coastal path to Shanklin. Those favouring a slightly easier route can cover the same journey along the Esplanade.

fine collection of tigers. Nearby is the excellent Dinosaur Museum, shaped like a giant pterodactyl, which opened in 2001. With interactive displays and the opportunity to watch experts working on recent finds, the museum is a must for anyone interested in prehistoric times. For those with more sporting inclinations, there is a pitch and putt course between the zoo and the museum.

The first church to be built in Sandown was Christ Church, which opened in the Broadway in 1845 and was much altered later in the century. Inside is the Princess Royal Chapel, named in honour of Queen Victoria's eldest daughter, who as well as becoming Empress of Germany (and mother of the last Kaiser, Wilhelm II) was a benefactor and frequent worshipper when staying in the town.

The growth of Sandown naturally led to demands for a second church and between 1875 and 1881 the Church of St John the Evangelist was built in Carter Street. Designed in the Victorian Gothic style and utilising local stone, it has some notable stained glass. Sandown also has two chapels: the red-brick Baptist in Station Avenue, and the stone and yellow brick Methodist in York Road – both of which were built in 1882.

Because of Sandown's long sandy beach it has always been regarded as a possible enemy landing place. Henry VIII ordered a fort erected on the beach, to the north of the pier. The fort never saw any action and neglect and decay together with coastal erosion lead to its demolition in 1631. It was replaced by a star-shaped second fort, which was built further inland in the 1630s (on the site of the present day Sandham Gardens). In 1811-15 a two-storey barrack block, with wings to house field guns, was erected on the site of what is now Sandham Leisure Centre. The central block, with its chequered red and white bricks, still survives behind the Centre. In due course the second fort suffered the same fate as the first, and was dismantled in the 1860s. A new battery was then built on the nearby cliff, which together with

SEAVIEW (G)

With its narrow High Street and alleys, weatherboarded houses and bay windows, Seaview retains much of the atmosphere and charm of a pre-1939 seaside resort. In the summer the streets are crowded with sailors, in winter all is peaceful and quiet.

The Caws family is mainly responsible for the present day village. In the 18th century John Caws and his wife Elizabeth, with their 12 children moved into the village. One son alone, Anthony, produced a further eight children. A mid 19th century directory list their occupations as ranging from coal merchant to lodging house keeper. At one point, there were seven ships' pilots with the name Caws.

The village developed rapidly in the last half of the 19th century, leading to calls for 'improvements' and better access. Finally it was decided to build a

pier to the design of another Caws, Frank, an architect and engineer, who modelled the result on a chain pier at Brighton. Seaview's 1000 feet long suspension chain pier opened in 1881, and was long enough for steamers to come alongside at all states of the tide. Alas, it now only survives in photographs. At the end of 1950, already in poor post-war condition, it was totally destroyed by gale force winds.

The view seawards down the High Street takes in No Man's Land Fort, one of four forts built out at sea and completed in 1880 to protect Portsmouth Harbour from attack.

The Church of St Peter was built in 1859 and although the interior is modest, it does have a fine Gothic style iron screen. The south aisle was added in 1921 as a war memorial chapel. Close by is the Beulah Free Church, which has a date stone of 1854.

Seaview's owes its sailing tradition to the Seaview Yacht Club, founded in 1893 with its clubhouse in a local hotel. In 1900 the club moved to its present site down on the shore, near the High Street. Seven years later it commissioned the building of the famous Mermaid class yachts – a fleet of one design 26 feet keelboats which are owned by the Club. Equally famous are the wooden clinker-built 12 feet Seaview One Design dinghies built locally in a yard near the Yacht Club. Their multi-coloured sails are a prominent feature of the annual August regatta.

There are several enjoyable walks starting at Seaview, including one along the recently rebuilt sea wall to Springvale, which lies halfway between the village and Ryde. Before reaching Springvale, you pass Saltern Cottages of 1640 – all whitewash, tiny dormer windows, and outsize sloping red tile roofs. In 1790 they were bought by the banker James Kirkpatrick, who after damming Barnsley Creek and embanking the Duver created salt pans. The cottages are where he housed his

ABOVE *Seaview, Saltern Cottages of 1640 were originally built to house workers at the nearby salt pans.*

TOP LEFT *Seaview. An old photograph of the chain pier, destroyed in 1950.*

ABOVE LEFT *Seaview, the High Street.*

TOP RIGHT *Seaview. The Beulah Free Church of 1854.*

workers, whilst the salt was used for salting down pork for the navy.

Much of what was once the salt pans is now Hersey Nature Reserve, a wetland reserve with a hide and good for waders and overwintering wildfowl.

At Springvale, in Oakhill Road, is the Seaview Wildlife Encounter, a bird sanctuary where visitors can see a wide variety of birds. A particular attraction is feeding time for the penguins, which is always a delight for children.

Further on towards Ryde, beyond the Battery Hotel, is Puckpool Park, which was the site of a gun battery built between 1863-65 and used as a training barracks during the Second World War. The area is now a public park, with a bowling green, tennis courts, children's play area, crazy golf and a café.

There is another excellent walk eastwards from Seaview to Seagrove Bay, where the Esplanade has recently been rebuilt, offering a fine walk to the National Trust copse at Horestone Point. To the east of the copse is the sandy beach of Priory Bay, whilst the coastal path continues round Nodes Point to St Helens.

SHALFLEET (E)

The village lies on the busy main Newport to Yarmouth road, and was small until new homes were built on its western edge. Despite the traffic, it still retains its own character – and all the constituent parts that help define our notion of a village: manor house, thatched cottages, mill, malthouse, inn, ancient vicarage, farm and attendant buildings.

The Caul Bourne flows through the village and, to the north of the bridge, widens into the shallow creek that gave Shalfleet its name and is a popular mooring for yachtsmen.

The old parish, which spanned the breadth of the Island and reached both north and south shores, was very rural and included Hamstead (*see* Hamstead).

In the middle of the village is the Church of St Michael the Archangel, dominated at its western end by the Norman tower. With its mighty five foot thick walls, the tower was undoubtedly a place of refuge for villagers taking shelter from French raiders during the Middle Ages, and access to the church through the tower has only been possible since the 19th century. The tower had a cupola added in the 18th century, and later a wooden steeple, both of which were long ago removed. Above the north door is an indistinct tympanum; perhaps of Daniel and two lions, perhaps David with a lion and bear. Inside, there is a Jacobean pulpit, box pews and some fine memorials. In

Shalfleet, the Church of St Michael the Archangel, showing the massive 5 feet thick tower walls.

the south wall in the south aisle are three 13th century windows which have some unusual oval tracery. The reredos was made in 1908, and incorporates wood from an Elizabethan communion table, linen-fold panelling, and H.M.S. *Nettle*, one of England's 'wooden walls'. The lovely tapestry curtains were embroidered by a local woman in memory of a former churchwarden.

Behind the church there is an open green space and a right of way leading south to Newbridge. There is a pleasant and easy walk from the New Inn north past the National Trust car park to Shalfleet Quay. Here yachts are brought ashore for overhauling and on a fine day there are some splendid views across the creeks and marshes towards the Solent and Newtown.

ABOVE *Shalfleet Manor in 1971.*   BELOW *Shalfleet Creek and Quay.*

Enjoy the High Ground

One of the keys to appreciating the Isle of Wight is to climb as high as possible and savour its spectacular views. Usually, the walker is rewarded with at least a glimpse of the sea. Access to the downland is easy with many roads, lanes and footpaths running along or across the high areas.

Starting at the east end of the Island, cars and walkers are able to climb Bembridge Down (341 feet, 104 metres), past the old fort, and on to the ridge. (Curiously 'down' is the ancient word used in southern England to describe an open expanse of chalk upland.) The down is broad and open, with ample space to enjoy the views to the north across Bembridge Harbour to the Solent and on to Portsmouth and beyond. To the south the views extend across Sandown Bay to Shanklin Down. At the far eastern end of the road is the Second World War artillery battery on top of Culver Cliff, an excellent site to explore.

Leaving Bembridge Down, drive westwards through Yarbridge and then up again on to Brading Down. Once again, there is plenty of space for parking, as well as a chance to sample more extensive views to the south across the valley below towards Shanklin Down, St Boniface Down and the south of the Island. A short distance west of the Brading Down view point and on the other side of the road is a small lay-by. From here the views stretch across the northern half of the Island towards the entrance to Southampton Water.

Proceeding westwards again over Ashey Down (426 feet, 130 metres) note the black and white sea mark on your right. It was erected in 1735 on the site of an old windmill. Adjacent stood a semaphore signalling station which relayed signals from naval shipping to Portsmouth dockyard. The next vantage point is a roadside lay-by on top of Mersley Down. From here, there are fine views to the south across the Arreton Valley. The intensive agriculture and horticulture of this fertile valley is laid before you, with acres of glasshouses glinting in the sun.

At any of these view-points it is worth getting out of the car and exploring even a short distance of the Downland Way footpath, which runs along the ridge parallel to the road and ends at Downend. Because of the extensive views across the centre of the Island the path is popular with walkers. To the south of the Hare and Hounds public house, from a lay-by and through a kissing gate, there is access on to Arreton Down (410 feet, 125 metres) with further, ever-changing views across the village of Arreton and the valley.

Additional vantage points to the west also provide views of this half of the Island. From the B3401 to the west of Calbourne are views to the north across Parkhurst Forest, as well as the Solent and New Forest.

The best views of the west of the Island require

Magnficent views can be enjoyed from the Tennyson Monument on Tennyson Down.

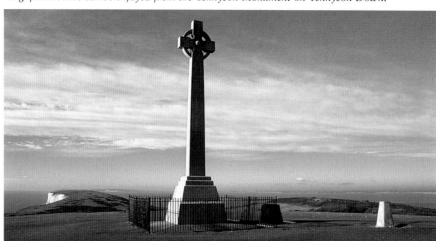

The crest of St Boniface Down, Ventnor.

more effort, as some of the downland is accessible only from footpaths, but the extra exertion is well rewarded. A short walk from the National Trust car park onto Mottistone Down (from the Calbourne to Brighstone road) allows enjoyment of a view that opens out the higher one climbs. From the top of the down (669 feet, 204 metres) there is a fine view across to Yarmouth and Freshwater.

One of the most impressive views is to be gained by climbing Tennyson Down from Freshwater Bay up to the Tennyson Monument (482 feet, 147 metres) and beyond. The views take in much of the Island, but also across to southern Hampshire and even, on a clear day, to Swanage and Old Harry Rocks (which are a continuation of the same chalk ridge).

The highest point on the Island is St Boniface Down (787 feet, 240 metres). The down is accessible by car from a steep narrow road from Lowtherville to the north-west of Ventnor. From here the views are panoramic, extending across the Island and to the Hampshire and Sussex coasts. Another spot not to be missed is St Catherine's Down (777 feet, 237 metres). This is reached from the car park on the south side of the Blackgang to Niton road (*see* Blackgang for details of St Catherine's Oratory). At the north end of the down is the Hoy Monument (*see* Chale). Given clear weather the steady climb from the car park to the top of the down is rewarded with breathtaking views.

For those happier with a more leisurely outing, there is an open-top bus trip from Yarmouth to Alum Bay and then out to the western extremity of the Island, the Old Needles Battery (National Trust). The ride aloft on the open-top bus on a narrow road, which seems at times perilously near to the cliff edge, is a delight. An alternative to the return journey is the walk across the downland from the Needles, heading eastwards past the Tennyson Memorial, and dropping down into Freshwater Bay where a bus will take you back to Yarmouth.

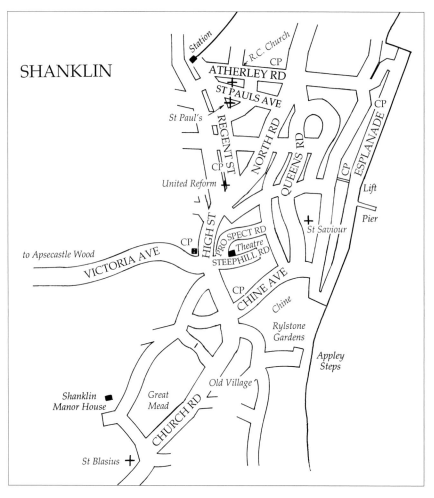

SHANKLIN

SHANKLIN (J)

The arrival of the railway in 1864 initiated the transformation of Shanklin from a church, two hotels, an inn and several cottages into a bustling Victorian seaside resort. In 1821 the population was a mere 155, 50 years later it had risen to 1,432.

Shanklin shares the large bay on the south-east of the Island with Sandown, but while it has less to offer than its neighbour in terms of attractions, it is ideal for those seeking a quiet, relaxing holiday. With its fine Victorian buildings and green open spaces, Shanklin has a charm all of its own.

The first port of call is the Chine – a deep, narrow ravine cut into the soft rock by water – which was first developed for the benefit of tourists in 1817. The original village was clustered around the head of the Chine, and is today known as Shanklin Old Village. The old Chine Inn was noted as a haunt for smugglers.

In the Second World War a pumping station hidden in the ruins of a bombed-out Shanklin hotel became the terminal for PLUTO, a pipeline laid under the Solent to Thorness and then underground across the Island. After D-Day and the Normandy Landings it was extended 80 miles under the Channel to Cherbourg, providing 56,000 gallons of fuel a day for the Allies. A short 65 yard section of pipeline still remains in the Chine, which is open throughout the summer and whose other attractions include a waterfall, rare plants, a Victorian tea garden and a heritage centre.

Next to the Chine is the extremely attractive Rylstone Gardens, which are open to the public, and whose trees and shrubs hide Rylstone Manor (built in 1863 and now a hotel), whose gables, Gothic style windows and elaborate chimneys are perfect Victorian picturesque.

For those seeking sea and sand, there are several ways down to the beach, including a Cliff Lift that was first

Shanklin. The entrance to the Chine.

ABOVE *Shanklin Old Village.*

RIGHT *Shanklin Cliff Lift.*

opened in 1891 and rebuilt after the Second World War. The 1000 feet long pier opened the same year, but succumbed to a storm in 1987, four years before its centenary. The seafront Esplanade has an array of small hotels, cafés, and amusements, including a putting green and crazy golf.

Although it was sea-bathing that primarily attracted visitors to Shanklin in the mid 19th century, it also had three mineral springs. The springs had first been discovered by a physician to Charles II, one of which by 1870 had been piped into a grotto for the benefit of the guests at the newly built Royal Spa Hotel at the bottom of Osborne Steps. The Fisherman's Cottage, at the foot of the Chine, offered hot and cold baths for those who had been bathing in the sea.

There is a pleasant walk through the Old Village – with its thatched cottages and gift shops. One of the more prominent houses is Vernon Cottage of 1817. Continue the walk to Great Mead, a large open area of grass with a pond and lined by trees that leads up to the parish Church of St Blasius.

The church was extensively rebuilt between 1852-59, but inside is the chest which once belonged to Thomas Silksted, prior of St Swithin's in Winchester, and bears the date 1512. Near to St Blasius is the manor house, built in the 19th century on the site of an earlier building and now the Manor Hotel.

Shanklin has two other Church of England churches – St Saviour in Queens Road (built from 1869 with the tower and spire added in 1887) and St Paul in Regent Street (1875-76) – as well as the 1950s Roman Catholic church in Atherley Road. However, the church most widely seen by visitors is

Shanklin, Pencil Cottage in the centre of the Old Village.

Shanklin Esplanade.

probably the 1883 United Reformed Church, which, with its clock tower, is in the town centre in the High Street. A stray wartime German bomb damaged the clock tower and it was rebuilt in the mid-1950s. There is also a Methodist chapel of 1864 in Regent Street.

At the junction of Steephill and Prospect Road is Shanklin Theatre, which began life as an institute in 1879 and later saw service as the Town Hall. Today it is a popular entertainment venue that stages productions throughout the year.

Visitors to Shanklin include the poet John Keats (1795-1821) (*see* Writers and Poets), whose two visits are commemorated in Keats Green. Later, in 1868, the American poet Henry Longfellow (1807-1882) stayed at the Crab Inn. His visit is remembered by a fountain bearing both the Union flag and Stars and Stripes and a brief verse noting that its waters flow 'for rich and poor the same'.

There are several excellent walks around the town, including along the Esplanade north to Sandown and back along the cliff path. Apsecastle Wood, to the west of Shanklin, is also an attractive destination for walkers.

SHORWELL (E)

One of the most interesting and unusual villages on the Island, Shorwell lies to the south of Rowborough and Cheverton Downs. What marks it out as particularly distinctive is that it has – either in the village or nearby – three manor houses.

On entering the village from the north you pass under a rustic wooden bridge, which links several public footpaths. On the right is the imposing North Court,

which is occasionally open to the public. The house was originally started by Sir John Leigh in 1615, who despite being partially paralysed played a central role in late Elizabethan Island life and died aged 83 in 1629. On the road to Limerstone is West Court, which is mainly early Tudor with Jacobean extensions and for many years was owned by another influential Island family, the Lisles. Finally, to the south, is the Elizabethan Wolverton Manor, which opens to the public about twice a year and stands near the site of an earlier house, the remains of whose moat can still be seen.

In the centre of the village, on the slope above North Court, is the Church of St Peter, parts of which are medieval. The writer Simon Jenkins has described its interior as being 'as fussily decorated as an Indian restaurant', but there is much of interest. Its prize is a St Christopher wall painting of about 1440 over the north door, but there is also a rare preaching pulpit. The monuments to the Leigh family are in the north chapel. Sir John is shown kneeling with his infant great grandson, who died at much the same time, and there is a fine more classical monument of 1619 to Elizabeth Leigh. The poppy-

Shorwell. The rustic bridge which spans the road down into the village.

heads on the bench ends were carved by Sir James Willoughby Gordon, who also gave the altar in the south aisle. Sir James was Wellington's Quartermaster General, and his failure to keep the army supplied with rations led to the loss of 2,000 lives and one of the worst disasters of the Peninsular War.

On the road to Kingston is the Methodist chapel of 1860 (enlarged 1880). Shorwell is rich in old and well built cottages. Fine Lane is well worth a stroll.

THORLEY (D)

The old village was centred around the 13th century Church of St Swithun and the once navigable Thorley Creek. By Victorian times the creek had long since silted up, the church was in need of repair, and the village had developed further to the east, along the road to Wellow.

All that remains of the church today is the lower part of the south porch, which was used as a mortuary chapel from 1871, surrounded by a graveyard

containing some fine table-top tombs. Near the door is an open stone coffin, in which bodies awaiting burial were once laid. A stone commemorates Thomas Urry, who died on Christmas Day 1631 aged 83, ending with the couplet: 'His aged years were almost twelve times seven/He's called to keep his Christmas now in heaven'.

The present Thorley Manor is one of the landmarks of West Wight. It was built in 1712, and is said to be the fifth building on this ancient site. It is a

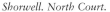
Shorwell. North Court.

Shorwell. Wolverton Manor and its grounds are the site of an annual fair.

Thorley. The remains of the old church.

Thorley. The manor house of 1712.

perfect 'Queen Anne' style house, with a hipped roof and four tall chimney stacks. It was built for Henry Holmes, the nephew of Sir Robert Holmes (*see* Yarmouth).

The replacement church of St Swithun was built in Thorley Street in 1871, about half-a-mile from the old one and near where most of the villagers lived. It was designed by a Newport architect, William Stratton, who saved the font and a Jacobean table from the old church, and installed them in the new one.

To the east of the manor house is the old brick and stone school, erected in 1866 for 90 pupils.

TOTLAND (D)

In 1870 the Totland Bay Estate Company was formed with ambitious plans to create a new seaside resort. Jenkinson's contemporary *Guide to the Isle of Wight* (1876) defined the Bay's attractions as 'beautiful smooth sands suitable for bathing and bathing machines'. To meet the anticipated

demand in what was then a fishing hamlet, a new road was built connecting Totland Bay, Colwell and Yarmouth.

By 1880 the company had erected a 450 feet long cast-iron pier. Overlooking it, was built the Totland Bay Hotel, which proved to be so popular that five years later it had to be enlarged. The pier survives, but not the hotel. Lodging houses and a bathing establishment with library and reading room were also built.

These developments turned Totland

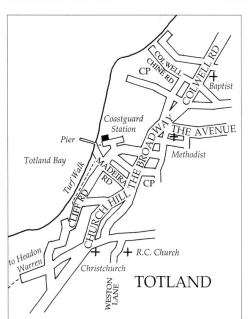

Totland. An old photograph of the Totland Bay Hotel from the pier. Built in about 1880, the hotel was demolished after the Second World War.

Totland Bay, showing the pier and Fort Albert.

Totland Pier.

Bay into a flourishing little seaside resort, which together with the sheltered character of the area, attracted wealthy Victorians to build red brick villas whose towers and gables remain a Totland feature today: there are several examples in Madeira Road.

Christchurch, Church Road, was built in 1875, with later additions. The interior is light and spacious. On the south wall is a memorial to the men of the parish who were killed in the First World War. The large lychgate was constructed from timbers from H.M.S. *Thunderer*, a veteran of Trafalgar.

On Weston Lane, in red brick in the Italian Romanesque style, is the 1923 Roman Catholic Church of St Saviour. In the Avenue is Totland Bay Methodist Church, erected in 1904 as a memorial church to Mary Toms and William Baily, the first Bible Christian missionaries to visit the Island (in 1823). The building to the rear is the Sunday School room.

From here a lane leads down to the Bay and pier, where in days gone by crowds of holiday makers landed from the steamers that once called. After the Second World War the pier was repaired and reopened. For some years Trinity House pilot service used it to land and pick up pilots to assist shipping in navigating the western Solent. Today it is in private hands and closed.

Totland takes its name from 'toutland', meaning 'look-out', making it an obvious site for a lifeboat station. In 1870, after the money had been raised by local Sunday school children, one duly opened at the south end of the Bay. In 1915 the Totland Lifeboat Station was equipped with the Island's first steam lifeboat. The station closed in 1924, but part of the 1884 boathouse still stands.

Today Totland is a suburb of Freshwater, but is well worth a visit. From the west end of Madeira Road a left hand turn takes you into Turf Walk and Cliff Road, from where there are splendid views across the western Solent from the Needles to Hurst Castle.

On a fine day there is an excellent walk from Totland to Alum Bay, also with fine seaward views. In late summer the flowering heather covering Headon Warren is another attraction. The Warren is also the site of one of the few Bronze Age burial mounds on the Island, dating to about 1500 BC.

A third walk leads north along the coast to Warden Point and Colwell Bay, where, at Cliff End, Fort Albert can be seen close to the water's edge. The large square red brick fort was built in 1854-56 to defend the Needles Passage, and today is divided into apartments.

UNDERCLIFF (I)

One of the Island's most beautiful stretches of landscape, runing for 7 miles from Dunnose to Blackgang, passing through Bonchurch, Ventnor, St Lawrence and Niton Undercliff (*also see colour section*).

The Undercliff is really a series of collapsed plateaus and terraces between the inner cliff and the sea cliff, some nearly half-a-mile wide, and can be seen at its best between Ventnor and Niton. The lower, or, sea cliff, is irregular in height, rising between 20 and 100 feet. The inner cliff is steep, in places rising 300 feet. Because the Undercliff is

sheltered and heavily wooded, it supports a rich early-flowering flora (perhaps easiest seen at Ventnor Botanic Gardens at Steephill).

The Undercliff owes its existence to Gault Clay, an impermeable plastic blue-grey silty mud, known locally as 'blue slipper'. When lubricated by seeping groundwater sitting on the surface of the clay, the inner cliff (of Upper Greensand capped with Chalk) become unstable, slumping forward and leading to huge landslips. Heavy falls have been recorded in 1799, 1818, 1847 and 1928.

Despite the Undercliff's instability, when wealthy members of the upper class started to tour the Island in the late 18th century it was the Undercliff that most attracted them. Henry Wyndham, describing it in 1793, wrote: 'If the mind of any person can remain tranquil on the first view of this wonderful country, or if he can gaze with indifference on the sublime scene above and below him, I do not envy the cool phlegm of his constitution, but I should advise him, to confine his future airings to the level of dusty roads that surround our metropolis'.

As marine villas and cottages became fashionable residencies for the gentry, new houses started to appear amongst

ABOVE *A view of the Undercliff, here showing Bonchurch and Ventnor. The seven-mile-long Undercliff forms a series of collapsed terraces between Dunnose and Blackgang.*

BELOW *Undercliff. The castellated Steephill Castle, built between 1833-35 by John Hambrough at a cost of about of £250,000 (today nearer £20 million), and demolished in 1963.*

the oaks and wild shrubs in the Undercliff. Tucked away in the trees, on both sides of the main road, are a succession of large private houses built in the late 18th or early 19th century. Perhaps the earliest rustic cottage in the area was the one built at Steephill for Hans Stanley, appointed Governor of the Isle of Wight in 1774. This, together with Steephill village and a popular inn kept by a Mrs Groves, was swept away when John Hambrough purchased the land to build the castellated Steephill Castle in 1833-35 (demolished in 1963 to make way for housing).

The best way to enjoy all the Undercliff has to offer architecturally is to take the footpath along the edge of the inner cliff, where you can look down on the houses. Old Park (now an hotel) was built in the early 19th century and enlarged by General Sir John Cheape after his return from India. It was later the home of the German industrial chemist William Spindler, who bought the estate in 1882 (*see also* St Lawrence). The next house and estate is 'Mirables', built in 1790 on the site of an earlier building for George Arnold, who had been a Gentleman of the Privy Chamber to George III. Next door is 'The Orchards', once owned by General Sir James Willoughby Gordon, a military secretary to the Duke of York (*see also* Shorwell).

There is public access to Reeth Bay, Binnel Point and Woody Point.

VENTNOR (I)

The town's history was shaped by an event outside its control, the publication, in 1829, of *The Influence of Climate in the Prevention and Curse of Chronic Diseases* by Sir James Clark, later a doctor to Queen Victoria. In his book, Clark described Ventnor as the perfect convalescent retreat. He pointed out that it was completely sheltered from the north and west winds while at the same time being open to the south. Dubbed the 'English Madeira', Ventnor was swiftly transformed into a

Ventnor, the third pier; completed in 1887 and named Royal Victoria Pier.

fashionable health resort from what had previously been no more than a hamlet comprising a waterfall and a few fishermen's cottages.

Despite Ventnor's rise, there have been some notable casualties. The town's first pier lasted four years from 1863. The second opened in 1872, but that too fell victim to storms and lack of finance. A third pier, the Royal Victoria, opened in 1887 – its arrival coincidentally marking the beginning of Ventnor's most prosperous period. In 1940, as an anti-invasion measure, the

Ventnor, looking out from the viewpoint.

centre section was removed. A new 683 feet long pier was built in the early 1950s, but that suffered the fate of its predecessors. First closed as unsafe, in 1993 it was demolished.

The story of the railway is much the same. Ventnor's first station opened in 1866 with the arrival of the line from Shanklin. It was followed in 1900 by Ventnor West, but both stations have long since closed: in 1966 and 1952 respectively.

The town's Victorian expansion shaped its character, providing much of what survives today. The catalyst was a parliamentary act of 1844, which led to lighting, paving, new roads, and the creation of the Esplanade.

Today, the town is built on a series of

Ventnor. These two engravings almost precisely overlap, and form a fine portrait of the mid 19th century town, showing how quickly it grew from a small hamlet into a fashionable resort.

terraces that rise up from the shoreline to the foot of the holm oak-covered St Boniface Down. The various street levels are linked by zig-zag roads, whilst the Esplanade has beach huts, a paddling pool, cafés and a car park (*see also colour section*).

On the road to the Esplanade is the Winter Gardens Pavilion, a 1930s building with wonderful views over the Bay from the café, as well as a

programme of entertainment. Across the road is the Cascade, a sub-tropical garden overlooking the sea front, where water from the old millstream plunges down the rock face and into the sea. The gardens, which are beautiful and well worth viewing, were laid out under the supervision of Edgar Haevey, the town surveyor in 1903.

On the site of the pier is the viewpoint, constructed in 2002 to disguise the waste water pumping station, and adjoining it is a small harbour – Ventnor Haven – which opened in 2003 and is the only mooring facility for yachts on the Island's south coast.

Halfway along the Esplanade, among the cafés and amusement arcades, is the Longshoreman's Museum – a small local historical and nautical museum with a collection of old engravings, photographs and models. A second museum of equal interest is the Ventnor Local History Museum in Spring Hill, whose displays reflect the area's history and which is open throughout the summer.

Near the Esplanade is the shelter and viewpoint. Climb up for the views and the markings on the floor indicating the points of the compass and distances to various places – London 125 km, Cardiff 174 km, Paris 317 km.

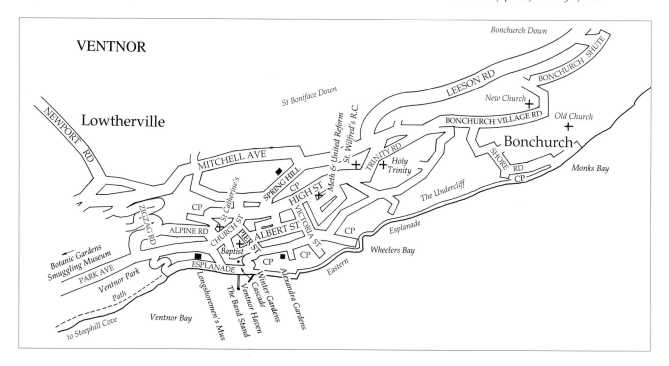

ABOVE *Ventnor. An aerial view of the town with the Downs behind, and a small but compact beach in the foreground.*

RIGHT *Ventnor, the Cascade.*

BELOW RIGHT *Ventnor Park, on the west side of the town and well worth visiting.*

With some fine Victorian houses built of local stone, Ventnor merits an architectural stroll. At the top of the town, in Mitchell Avenue, is Huish Terrace, originally built in the mid 19th century to provide holiday homes for church workers from the London City Mission. In Albert Street is all that remains of the former Town Hall of 1878. The fine classical façade has been saved, but is now the frontage to a block of flats.

Ventnor's mild climate has attracted its fair share of distinguished people. The historian Lord Macaulay, who stayed at Madeira Hall in 1850, summed up its pleasures: 'Here I am,' he wrote, 'lodged most delightfully. I look out on one side to the crags and myrtles of the Undercliff . . . On the other I have a view of the sea, which at this moment is as blue as the sky, and as calm as the Serpentine.' A less likely visitor was Karl Marx, who stayed at 1 St Boniface

Ventnor. The Royal National Hospital for Consumption opened in 1869 and closed in 1964. The Botanic Gardens now occupy the site.

balconies facing south out to sea so that the patients benefited from the fresh air. With the improvement in medicine the hospital became obsolete and it closed in 1964 and was afterwards demolished. The Botanic Gardens were formed in the former hospital gardens.

From the car park it is a short walk down to Steephill Cove, which offers a small but excellent beach for those wishing to spend a day enjoying the sun.

Gardens in 1881 and 1882-83. As a young lad, Winston Churchill spent August 1880 in Wheeler's Bay Road with his nanny's sister. A year later Edward Elgar spent part of his honeymoon at 3 Alexander Gardens.

The first church to be built in Ventnor was St Catherine's in Church Street and its construction, in 1836-37, owed much to the patronage of John Hambrough, a local landowner who lived at Steephill Castle and lies buried in the church vaults. The church, which lost its spire in 1921 when it was deemed unsafe, is a few yards from the bustle of the town centre and offers a haven of peace and tranquillity. The other Church of England church is Holy Trinity, built in Trinity Road in 1860-62, which retains its fine spire, despite an alarm in the early 1980s when it became clear that the spire required expensive repairs. However, when it

was discovered that the cost of removing the spire was greater than for the repairs, the money was raised and the work carried out. The interior is illuminated by beautiful Victorian stained-glass windows, the work of the noted Clayton and Bell factory.

The Roman Catholic Church – St Wilfrid's – is also in Trinity Road and was built in 1871. The Baptist Chapel is four years older and can be found in Pier Street, while the Ventnor United Church – the result of a 1976 union between the Methodist and United Reform churches – is in the High Street. The building was originally opened in 1861 as a Wesleyan Methodist Chapel.

Thanks to the Esplanade linking Ventnor to Bonchurch, it is possible to complete a circular walk via Shore Road and through Bonchurch village. Another pleasant walk is along the coastal path from the Esplanade to Steephill Cove, which takes in Ventnor Park. The park is attractively laid out with flower beds, shrubs and a stream. The next place of interest is Ventnor Botanic Gardens, a 27-acre, sub-tropical garden with a temperate house, visitor centre, gift shop and café as well as plenty of parking. Admission is free and it is quite easy to spend a morning here, strolling around the splendid gardens.

The former Royal National Hospital for Consumption occupied the whole of today's car park. The hospital opened in 1869 and expanded until there were eleven blocks with a chapel forming the central portion. All blocks had open

WELLOW (E)

Just two roads – Thorley Street and Top Road – go to make the hamlet of Wellow. The street has some attractive stone and brick cottages of varying ages and on the south side of the centre of the hamlet is Millennium Green, which has a mosaic featuring the name of the trustees of the projects and those who contributed to its cost. Also in the street is the Baptist Chapel. Built in the early 19th century and enlarged in 1902, there is a small, well-kept burial ground to the rear.

At the junction with Top Road there is an air raid warden's hut surviving from the Second World War and, in the road itself, is the Wellow Literary Institute, built in 1893 and still very much in use by the villagers today as a meeting hall. The clock in the gable was unveiled in 1907 by Sir Godfrey Baring, the Island's MP.

Wellow, a cottage near the Green.

Wellow. The Second World War air raid warden's shelter at the junction with Top Road.

Queen Victoria and the Island

Queen Victoria and her husband landed on the Island, at East Cowes, in August 1843, and stayed only a few hours. Whilst this was Prince Albert's first visit it was the Queen's third.

Her first visit (as Princess Victoria) was with her mother, the Duchess of Kent, in 1831. They landed at Ryde Pier and went by carriage to Norris Castle, near East Cowes, which they had taken for the season. Besides local carriage rides and attending Whippingham Church, they visited Newport, and Cowes. On 14th September the Princess laid the foundation stone of St James's Church in East Cowes. Their visit ended a month later.

The next visit came in July 1833. Again they stayed at Norris Castle, but this time it was used more as a base for excursions to other parts of the Island and to the mainland. The Duchess and her daughter paid a return visit to St James's Church, this time to attend the consecration service. In answer to an invitation from the Earl of Yarborough they sailed round the Island to the south coast to call on the Earl at his cottage at St Lawrence. During the visit they saw a demonstration of Mr Dennett's rockets for saving lives from shipwrecks. In the first week of November they sailed to Southampton on their return to Kensington Palace.

In 1843 the Queen and Prince Albert were on their way to visit the French king and queen, when they landed at Cowes from the Royal Yacht *Victoria and Albert*. A carriage took them to Norris Castle, where they stayed for a few hours. The Queen then took her husband on a tour of East Cowes before returning to their yacht.

Although this first visit together was fleeting, it helped Queen Victoria and Prince Albert decide that they needed a place of their own, away from the Court and London life. They both agreed that the Isle of Wight might be suitable, and with its treasured memories of earlier visits by the Queen East Cowes in particular was considered ideal.

Osborne House, owned by Lady Isabella Blachford, was for sale. Before being committed to

An 1897 Diamond Jubilee photograph of Queen Victoria.

a purchase the Queen leased the estate for a year with an option to buy from March 1844. The stay was successful and it was decided that the property should be bought. The asking price was £30,000, but after negotiations it was secured for £26,000 in May 1845. Also purchased was the neighbouring Barton Estate for a further £18,600. In total, with other purchases of smaller parcels of land the estate amounted to 2,000 acres. Within days of moving in the Queen was writing to Lord Melbourne about how delighted she was with her new home and how beautiful were the valleys, woods and views of the sea.

At first the royal couple intended to improve and make additions to the Georgian Osborne House, but finally they concluded that a new house would be both better and cheaper. The Prince Consort

Osborne House, which the Queen purchased in 1845 and was later demolished.

ABOVE *The Queen's Sitting Room. Her desk is on the left next to that of Prince Albert.*

BELOW *Queen Victoria died aged 81 on a small couch in this bedroom on January 17, 1901.*

collaborated with the London builder-contractor, Thomas Cubitt, and together they designed the new house. Construction started in June 1845 and finished in 1851. The Queen paid the last visit to the old house in December 1847 and shortly afterwards it was demolished.

The result of the collaboration between Prince Albert and Thomas Cubitt was a grand Italianate villa positioned to offer fine views down across the parkland to the sea. Cast-iron girders were

ABOVE *Osborne House, the Royal Apartments are on the right, the Main Wing on the left.*

RIGHT *An old photograph of Swiss Cottage.*

BELOW *An 1880 engraving of the Queen at her desk being entertained at the piano by her daughter Princess Beatrice.*

incorporatd to give the house strength, which when finished consisted of four wings: the Pavilion Wing (of private apartments) completed in 1846; the Household Wing in 1848; the Main Wing in 1851; and the later Durbar Wing, built in 1890-1891 to celebrate the Queen becoming Empress of India.

Prince Albert's appetite for 'improvements' was much in evidence. The gardens, terraces and

grounds were largely his design: he marshalled his workforce from the top of the Flag Tower using a system of signal flags. One pleasure in which all the family shared was swimming in Osborne Bay. The royal bathing machine can still be seen at Osborne today, next to the Swiss Cottage in the grounds. The Swiss Cottage was built 1854-55 for the instruction and pleasure of the Royal children.

The Royal Household was usually in residence at Osborne for July and August, and again from December to February. Life at Osborne was relatively relaxed and the Royal Family enjoyed their visits. Prince Albert, when not working on the estate, enjoyed playing with his children. That the Queen was delighted with Osborne and her time there is clearly shown in her letters and diaries. All

The Durbar Room, built 1890-91, looking towards the Minstrel's Gallery.

this changed in December 1861 when the Prince died at Windsor. The Queen, bereft, retreated to Osborne and did not leave again until March 1862. She continued to stay at Osborne throughout the rest of her life for Christmas and much of the summer, implementing many of the improvements to the estate which had been planned by her husband. Towards the end of 1900 the Queen's health deteriorated, but she still came to Osborne for Christmas. On 17th January 1901 she suffered a stroke and died in the house on January 22nd aged 81 years.

The house and estate was left to Edward VII who, having no fondness for Osborne, gave it to the nation. He retained the Barton Estate and used it occasionally when entertaining: it was sold by George V in 1922. The Osborne Naval College was built in the grounds, but that also closed in the 1920s. Part of the house was opened to the public, and another part became a convalescent home.

Today Osborne House is open to the public. There is extensive access to the house, including the Main Wing, the Grand Corridor and Council Room. Also on view are the Royal Apartments which are furnished as at the time of Queen Victoria's residence. A high point of the visit must be the stunning Durbar Room, decorated in a highly ornate Indian style. The house stands in beautiful grounds with a formal terrace and walled fruit and flower garden. The Swiss Cottage is also open to the public along with its own garden which was worked by the Royal children. Nearby is the museum which was built to house the ever-growing collections of the children. There is also the Victoria and Albert barracks, built in 1856, with the help of the young Princes, for them to play in.

Today Osborne is managed by English Heritage and is a key visitor attraction on the Island. Anyone interested in the Victorian period or the history of the Royal Family will find a visit hugely rewarding. To take in all that is on offer one should allow a whole day for the visit and there is plenty to interest for all ages. A shop and refreshments are also available. The house and grounds are open from spring to late autumn.

WHIPPINGHAM (B)

A small, somewhat sprawling village, which nevertheless attracts many thousands of visitors every year, drawn to its unique and fascinating church.

Built between 1854 and 1861, St Mildred's, in Beatrice Avenue, is quite unlike any other church on the Island. Its highly distinctive architecture is a result of a partnership between the architect A.J. Humbert (architect of Sandringham and the mausoleum at Frogmore) and Prince Albert. Whippingham's close proximity to Osborne House meant that much of the surrounding land was owned by Queen Victoria, and St Mildred's is where the royal family worshipped when in residence on the Island.

The church, which is at least the third on the site, is therefore a must for anyone with an interest in Victorian royalty: the only relic of its past is a Saxon carving set in the west wall of the porch. Inside there is a royal pew and, opposite, the Battenberg Chapel. This contains the tombs of Queen Victoria's youngest (and favourite) child, Princess Beatrice, and her husband Prince Henry of Battenberg. Princess Beatrice (1857-1944) married Prince Henry of Battenberg in the church in 1885. Queen Victoria

Whippingham, the Church of St Mildred.

Whippingham, the Church of St Mildred. The Battenberg Chapel is on the left, behind the columns.

Princess Beatrice and Prince Henry of Battenberg, a honeymoon photograph, 1885.

ABOVE *Whippingham. The picturesque brick almshouses built opposite the church in 1875-76.*

BELOW *Whitecroft. This distinctive tower once held the water tanks for the County Lunatic Asylum, itself now mainly empty.*

WHITECROFT (F)

Lying south of Newport on the road to Chillerton, and not shown on the colour map, the hamlet consists of a farm and a few cottages and was largely unknown until 1894 when work began on the building of an asylum for the mentally ill, the County Lunatic Asylum. Until then patients had to travel to Knowle Hospital, in Fareham, for treatment. Today the hospital, built of bricks made locally, is mainly empty, the patients having moved to a new building beside St Mary's Hospital. The fine tower, however, can still be seen for miles around.

WHITWELL (I)

A small village with stone-built cottages in its main street while, to the west, there is a more recent development.

Visitors may be puzzled by the red iron pillars dotted around the village. They are water standards, complete with a stand for a bucket, and the cost of their installation in 1887 was met by William Spindler, of Old Park, St Lawrence (*see* St Lawrence).

Whitwell. One of several water standards paid for by William Spindler of Old Park to bring fresh drinking water to the village.

appointed him Governor of the Island, but he died of malaria in Africa in 1895 and his widow was appointed in his place. The Princess was much-loved by the Island, took a great interest in its affairs, and made Carisbrooke Castle her summer residence. She held her post until her death in 1944, remaining the Island's longest serving governor.

In the churchyard are the graves of Earl Mountbatten's parents, and the yachtsman and naval architect Uffa Fox (1898-1972), whose headstone depicts the airborne lifeboat he designed to help save the life of aircrews forced to land in the sea during the Second World War. In the car park is an exhibition hall containing displays about the history of the village and church.

Opposite the church are some attractive red brick almshouses, built 1875-76 on the site of an old farmyard to house Osborne Estate's aged labourers and their wives and widows. Today they belong to the local housing association.

Whippingham lies to the east of the River Medina and is on the road to East Cowes. Close to the road is Whippingham Heights, an estate of houses built on the site of a Second World War anti-aircraft gun battery. Opposite is the school, built in 1863-64 and designed by Prince Albert, opened by Queen Victoria in 1864. Members of the Royal Family visited the school several times. Nearby is a road that leads down to the Folly Inn – a riverside spot that is equally popular with visitors and yachtsman who use the moorings.

any time of the year, offering ancient oaks whose ancestors were part of a medieval hunting forest, coppiced chestnut, a carpet of bluebells in the spring and fine displays of autumn colour.

Frank Morey, a well-known local naturalist, bequeathed the first part of the copse to the Trust in 1926, followed by further donations of land from his sister Kathleen. It was again added to in 1985, making a total area of 50 acres.

WOOTTON BRIDGE (B)

In the past Wootton Bridge consisted of two communities; the parish of Wootton centred around the old church, and Wootton Bridge at the north end of the large parish of Arreton. Today the village straddles the main road between Ryde and Newport and the whole area is called Wootton Bridge to distinguish it from a number of other Woottons in England. The bridge, or causeway, that carries the main road, spans the creek and enjoys fine views on each side. To the north there are yachts and houseboats, to the south the millpond with the countryside and downs beyond.

The tide mill was first mentioned in 1364 when it was the property of Quarr Abbey. The mill which stood next to the Sloop Inn (once the miller's house), was demolished in 1962.

There is a Methodist Chapel in Station Road, opened in 1898 (its 1840 predecessor in the High Street is now

Wootton Bridge, the mill pond.

The church is unusual in that it has a twin dedication – to St Mary and St Rhadegund – a result of there being two separate chapels in one building. The present church dates mainly from the 16th century, when much was changed. The early 17th century pulpit is thought to be the work of a village craftsman.

There is a pleasant walk from the village up the lane, past the former railway station, to the hamlet of Nettlecombe, which sits on a hill overlooking Whitwell. Another good walk is to take the old road, now Ashknowle Lane, to Niton.

WINFORD (F)

Winford, which lies between Apse Heath and Alverstone, is a residential

area built since the Second World War.

Close by is Borthwood Copse, an area of ancient woodland now in the ownership of the National Trust. There are two small car parks with direct access to the copse and, with its network of paths, it is worth a visit at

WROXALL (I)

Wroxall, which lies to the north of Ventnor, would win no awards in a contest of the Island's most attractive villages, but it does occupy a lovely area with walks radiating out in all directions. The village first grew when the railway opened in 1866 and the station was built in its centre, but further expansion had to wait until after the railway closed in 1966 and more land became available.

Right in the centre of the village is the church of St John the Evangelist, built in 1877 with the clock tower and belfry added in 1911. Inside is a splendid oil painting called *From the Children of Their Church, Christmas 1941*, which is highly evocative of the spirit of Christmas. Nearby, on the main road, is the Methodist church, which was built in 1886 and is still in use today.

One of the most interesting of numerous walks is along Manor Road to Middle Barn Farm, which passes several farms and cottages plus the entrance to the old 1,312 yard railway tunnel under Wroxall and Littleton Downs.

To the west of the village lies the shell of what was once the grandest house of the Island – Appuldurcombe. The Worsley family secured the estate by marriage in Tudor times, and in 1690

closed). The High Street has a good selection of shops, and Minghella's, the well-known Island ice cream maker with a justifiably renowned product.

In Church Road, to the north of the village, is the ancient Church of St Edmund, a small Norman church originally a chapel for the nearby manor house. The church has a fine Norman doorway that leads into the nave. To the north are 12th century pillars either side of the arch leading into the Lady Chapel.

The manor of Wootton was held for many years by the Lisle family with the manor house standing close to the church, where Wootton Farm is today. Except for a black marble sepulchral slab commemorating the Sir William Lisle who returned here from exile with

TOP *Wootton Bridge, the Creek north of the causeway.*

ABOVE *Wootton Bridge, looking across the causeway towards Kite Hill.*

Charles II at the Restoration, there is no trace of their long association with the parish.

To the south, in Station Road, is St Marks Church, built in 1909 and designed by Percy Stone, an Island architect. Services are shared between the two churches.

Also in Station Road is the railway station, which is the farthest point westwards of the Isle of Wight Steam Railway. From spring to autumn there is a steam service to Havenstreet and beyond to Smallbrook interchange.

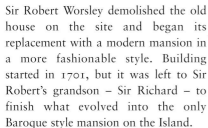

Yafford. The two most interesting houses in the hamlet are Yafford House (TOP) with its large 18th century extension forming a new frontage, and a new house which replicates an earlier one destroyed by a bomb in the Second World War.

Sir Robert Worsley demolished the old house on the site and began its replacement with a modern mansion in a more fashionable style. Building started in 1701, but it was left to Sir Robert's grandson – Sir Richard – to finish what evolved into the only Baroque style mansion on the Island.

The Worsley family were rich and powerful and filled the house with paintings and fine objects collected from abroad. When Sir Richard died in 1805, the estate passed to his niece, the wife of the first Earl of Yarborough. In 1855 the estate was sold and the house became a school – Dr Pound's Academy for Young Gentlemen. That closed in the 1890s and in 1901 Appuldurcombe became a temporary home for Benedictine monks. When they left in 1908 to build the new

ABOVE *Wroxall. Two views of Appuldurcombe House. The engraving shows it when occupied by the Worsley family, the photograph as a largely roofless ruin in the care of English Heritage.*

Quarr Abbey (*see* Binstead), it lay empty for a number of years. During the Second World War a landmine fell nearby causing substantial damage.

Today, the largely roofless but still striking ruins are in the care of English Heritage, and the house and grounds are well worth visiting for a flavour of the Georgian island at its grandest.

YAFFORD (E)
The hamlet lies to the south of Shorwell and is a scatter of picturesque old

cottages and modern houses among a maze of narrow roads.

There are two houses of particular interest – one old, the other new. The old one is Yafford House, which has a date stone of 1709 on the main wing. Later in the 18th century, in more affluent times, a three storey wing, built of cut stone and rendered sides, was added to the east end.

A short distance away at the junction of Chine and Mill Lanes is an attractive pond with spring flowers on its banks. Behind the pond is a new house built out of old stone in the style of a 17th century yeoman's farmhouse.

At the west end of the hamlet is Yafford water mill right beside the road. Built mainly of red brick, it still retains its wheel.

Writers and Poets

Some of the greatest names in English literature have, at one point or another, visited or taken up residence on the Isle of Wight, attracted by the tranquillity, scenery, clean air and a desire to escape from the hubbub of city life.

One of the earliest visitors came not from choice but because he was under arrest. William Davenport (1606-1668) was educated at Oxford and claimed that William Shakespeare, a frequent visitor to his father's inn, was his godson. Between 1629 and 1649 he published a number of works and became Poet Laureate in 1637. During the Civil War he supported the Royalist cause and was knighted by Charles I in 1643. Later, when threatened by the Parliamentarians with arrest, Davenport was forced to flee to France. He was commissioned by Queen Henrietta Maria to ship a group of settlers to Virginia. He was captured en route and in 1650 became a prisoner in Cowes Castle (now the Royal Yacht Squadron clubhouse) for several months. Here he wrote a large section of *Gondibert*, his most well-known poem. Soon, however, he was transferred to the Tower, thanks to the intervention of John Milton, from where the poem was published.

One celebrated early literary visitor was the poet John Keats (1796-1821), who arrived on the Island

The poet John Keats visited the Island twice.

Winterbourne House, Bonchurch, where Charles Dickens stayed in 1849.

in April 1817 after taking advice from his brother that the air would be beneficial to his health. At first, Keats lived at Eglantine Cottage, Shanklin, and, while he liked the area and the chine, he found he could not work without access to a library and soon moved to Carisbrooke. During his short stay he began work on one of his most important works, *Endymion*, published in 1818.

With his health deteriorating as a result of consumption, Keats returned to Eglantine Cottage in 1819 and wrote to friends of his enthusiasm for his lodgings and Shanklin. While he was there, he wrote the dialogue for the play, *Otho the Great*, and established a friendship with J.H. Reynolds, another of the Island's literary visitors. The two men had first met in 1816, two years after Reynolds had published two volumes of verse. Reynolds later studied law and came to the Isle of Wight to become clerk to the county court. Keats quickly tired of life in Shanklin – claiming he found the climate depressing – and moved to Winchester in August of 1819.

In July 1849 one of England's greatest writers came to stay at Bonchurch. Charles Dickens (1812-1870) rented 'Winterbourne' from July to the following October. He was in need of a long summer holiday, and the Undercliff proved the remedy he needed. There were rounders on the beach, lunch parties, visits to friends. Picnics on the downs were another attraction and Dickens thought that the views equalled those in the Mediterranean. Despite the diversions he did make progress with *David Copperfield* during his time on

Alfred Lord Tennyson, who lived for many years at Farringford House, Freshwater.

the Island, and it was to Shanklin that he later sent Mr and Mrs Lamlee for their unhappy honeymoon in *Our Mutual Friend*.

Perhaps the most famous poet to have connections with the Island is Alfred Lord Tennyson (1809-1892), who lived at Farringford House, Freshwater for 40 years. The success of his poem *Maud* and becoming Poet Laureate in 1850 enabled him to rent Farringford at £2 per week in 1853 and, as his fame and income continued to increase, he eventually bought the house for £6,900 three years later. It was in that year that the Prince Consort paid a surprise visit and vowed to bring Queen Victoria to see such an attractive part of the Island. Tennyson visited the Queen at Osborne several times and in 1884 she created him Baron Tennyson. He wrote many of his most famous works on the Isle of Wight, including *Charge of the Light Brigade*, *Enoch Arden* and *Idylls of the King*. However, he did not relish his celebrity and was unhappy at the large numbers of tourists visiting Farringford in order to get a glimpse of him. Accordingly, in 1868 he had Aldworth House built in Sussex and would then spend his summers there, returning to the Island for the winter months. He

died at Aldworth in 1892 and was buried at Westminster Abbey.

Another famous poet who found the Island to his liking was Algernon Swinburne (1837-1909). His parents moved to East Dene House at Bonchurch the year before his birth. Swinburne spent his childhood at Bonchurch and, after attending Eton and Oxford, formed a close attachment to his cousin, Mary Gordon, and would visit her regularly at her home at Northcourt, Shorwell. Mary had a huge influence over Swinburne and there are several references to her in his work, although their relationship ended in 1864 when she became engaged to Colonel Disney Leith. The poet spent the remainder of his life in Putney, but was buried beside members of his family in the churchyard of St Boniface Church, Bonchurch.

The Rev. C.L. Dodgson (1832-1898), better known as Lewis Carroll, first visited the Isle of Wight in June 1859 when, with a fellow cleric, he stayed at Plumbley's Hotel in Freshwater Bay. He tried, unsuccessfully, to penetrate the inner circle of Tennyson and Julia Margaret Cameron, the photographer. Carroll returned three years later but was successful only in securing an audience with one of Tennyson's sons. In 1864, however, he did manage to meet the poet but must have been dismayed to be bluntly told that Tennyson was no fan of his work. He did, though, manage to take a photograph of the poet's wife and their sons. His final visit to the Island, in 1871, came several years

The poet Algernon Swinburne lived with his parents at East Dene House, Bonchurch.

The writer and poet Alfred Noyes purchased Lisle Combe House, St Lawrence, in 1932.

after the publication of *Alice's Adventures in Wonderland* and *Through the Looking Glass*. He took rooms in Sandown and there wrote much of his nonsense verse, *The Hunting of the Snark*, which was published the following year.

Alfred Noyes (1880-1958), perhaps best known for his poem, *The Highwayman*, fell in love with Lisle Combe House at St Lawrence when he first saw it in 1929, but had to wait for three years before he could become its owner. He was particularly enchanted by the gardens and wrote about them in his book, *Orchard's Bay*, published in 1939. In that year he travelled to Rome to write about the election and coronation of a new pope. Noyes spent much of the next decade lecturing and reading from his work. Gradually he became blind and by the time he returned to Lisle Combe in 1949 he was unable to see his beloved garden, although he still claimed to gain enjoyment from the scent of the flowers. He died in 1958 and is buried in the Catholic cemetery at Freshwater.

Another well-known writer who made his name between the wars was J.B. Priestley (1894-1984), who brought his family to live at Billingham Manor House, north of Chale Green, in 1933. While in residence he wrote the novel, *Let The People Sing*, and several plays, including *Time And The Conways* and *An Inspector Calls* as well as an autobiographical work entitled *Rain Over Godshill*. His wartime work, which included talks for the BBC, kept him on the mainland, but he returned to Billingham in 1946 and, two years later, moved to

Brook Hill House at Brook. Among the work he produced there was *Festival At Farbridge*, a satirical novel that mocked several prominent residents of the Isle of Wight. In 1959 he sold the house and returned permanently to the mainland.

All the above were writers who grew to love the Island after paying visits, but Albert Midlane (1825-1909), author of around 400 hymns, was a local man. Born in Newport, he was an ironmonger by trade but began to write hymns as a child, although he was 19 before he had his first one accepted. Perhaps his most famous was *There's A Friend For Little Children*. In 1860 *Vecta's Garland*, his first book, was published, containing lyrics that praised the charms of the Island. This was followed by further books, including *Catechism of Carisbrooke Castle*, published in 1876.

The novelist and playwright J.B. Priestly with his wife Jane at Billingham Manor in 1940.

YARMOUTH (D)

The little picturesque town is the only port at the western end of the Island. It owes its rise to the gradual silting up of the creek to Thorley, and despite development inland and eastward, the town's nucleus remains compact and largely unspoilt. It has an attractive harbour, a castle, a fine church, a cluster of good 18th century town houses near the Square, good pubs, and there is much to see and enjoy.

Its history reflects its importance. The French raided it in 1377 and again, according to some historians, in 1524. The Crown also realized the town's importance by making it a borough in the 12th century, and – like nearby Newtown – Yarmouth regularly sent two members to Parliament right up to the passing of the 1832 Reform Act.

To put a stop to raids on the town

ABOVE *Yarmouth. An aerial view of the town with the pier and a ferry leaving for Lymington. To the right of the Quay is a row of 19th century buildings once occupied by Customs and other port offices.*

RIGHT *Yarmouth Castle.*

BELOW *Yarmouth Harbour and Quay.*

Henry VIII built a castle next to the quay, on 'King's Land' – and thus outside the jurisdiction of the borough. The work was overseen by Richard Worsley, then Captain of the Wight, and in 1547 £1,000 was paid to George Mills for the building works. Today the Castle is managed by English Heritage. The Long Room, master gunner's parlour and gun platform are all open to the public in the summer; and there are good views across the Solent from the ramparts.

Until the construction of the break-water between 1843-47 the Harbour

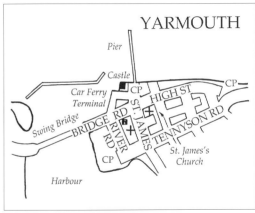

was open to the sea. Money to meet the cost was raised by various means by the Corporation: one local landowner, G.H. Ward, made a considerable donation, plus 5,000 tons of stone. Several hundred piles were given by the Admiralty from Portsmouth Dockyard. By the 1970s the breakwater was showing its age and in 1972 it was rebuilt. The first section of the new breakwater consists of the granite remnants left behind by the Americans after they had bought and dismantled the old London Bridge. They were shipped from the Thames, and arrived in such large pieces that they had to be broken up on the quay. The rest of the breakwater is of Portland stone – all of which is held in place by old railway rails which came from the dismantled Cowes to Newport railway line.

Before the construction of the old wooden harbour bridge, which opened in 1860, the River Yar was crossed by a ferry which beached on the sands at Norton. In the 1980s it was decided that a much larger bridge was needed, and the present one was opened in 1987 at a cost of £2.4 million. The centre section swivels open to allow vessels through.

The town itself is well worth exploring on foot. A good place to start is the George Hotel, next door to the Castle. The George was built as a town house in around 1700, and what is now its lawn was once the site of the home of a fabled 17th century Governor of the Isle of Wight, Sir Robert Holmes (1621-1692), whose memorial is in the church.

To the north of the Square is Yarmouth's famous wooden pier. The 685 feet pier was built in the 1870s to serve the ferries and excursion steamers. Over ten years from 1983 it was much

TOP *Yarmouth Town Hall.*

CENTRE *Yarmouth. The tower of St James's Church was built in two stages, the top half in 1831 as a seamark and memorial.*

BOTTOM *Yarmouth, the memorial to Sir Robert Holmes in St James's Church.*

restored using a hardwood less prone to saltwater worm. The new decking is inscribed with the names of those who donated money for the work. It is listed by English Heritage and is said to be the last wooden pier in England. To walk down the pier is a joy, with lovely views across to Lymington and the New Forest. In the summer excursion boats make trips to Lymington River, Hurst Castle, Keyhaven and round trips to the Needles. The entrance to the pier was rebuilt in 1927 and contains a popular café. To the east of the pier is the 1897 clubhouse of the Royal Solent Yacht Club, the work of the architect Sir Aston Webb (*see also* Brook).

Across the Square is the old red brick Town Hall which – according to the plaque – was rebuilt in 1763. The Square is lined with shops and leading off is the High Street, which has some of Yarmouth's finest 18th and 19th century houses.

On the south side of the Square is St James's Church which was built on the site of a previous church. Work began in 1635, but parishioners had to wait nearly 200 years for the tower to be completed. Note how the stone changes half-way up. The top part was finished in 1831, partly as a seamark for shipping, and partly as a memorial to his son, by Daniel Alexander, the architect responsible for Dartmoor Prison and Wapping docks.

The church is a place of tranquillity in the midst of the town. In the Holmes Chapel is a memorial to Sir Robert Holmes that, like the man himself, has a particularly colourful past. Holmes's rise as a soldier of fortune combines piracy, slave trading off west Africa, a spell in the Tower of London, loyalty to Charles II (who knighted him and who he entertained in Yarmouth), as well as undoubted courage and seamanship. The memorial in the church is there because Sir Robert captured a French ship carrying an unfinished statue of Louis XIV, together with its sculptor, whom he ordered to complete the work with a representation of his head rather than that of the French king.

Yarmouth, the former tide mill.

Holmes died a bachelor, and left his estate on the Island to his nephew, Henry, subject to the condition that he marry his illegitimate daughter Mary. The two did so, later producing 15 children – one of whom, Thomas, paid for the 1763 rebuilding of the Town Hall.

After leaving the church, a walk along Bridge Road passes the bus station from where, in the summer months, it is possible to take an open-top bus to Alum Bay and the Needles Fort. Close by is the Lifeboat Station,

Yaverland. The manor house.

which opened in 1924 with the Cowes-built *BASP* (a lifeboat whose curious name was concocted from the initial letters of the surnames of the first benefactors). Today's boat is the powerful Severn Class *Eric and Susan Hiscock*, named after a famous yachting couple who lived in Yarmouth and twice circumnavigated the globe.

Those happier on dry land can enjoy the nautical bustle of the Harbour, or the Lymington ferries coming and going. Celia Fiennes, the remarkable traveller, stepped ashore at Yarmouth in the late 17th century, as did the artist Thomas Rowlandson a century later.

A popular walk is along the route of the old railway line from Yarmouth to Freshwater. The path closely follows the river and there are excellent views across the estuary. Early in the walk the path passes the brick three storey tide mill of 1793. It is now a private house, and was once the summer home of the historian, A.J.P. Taylor.

At the south end of the walk turn right over the Causeway – note the Second World War pill box on the left. Beside Freshwater church is a marked footpath which proceeds north along the western bank of the river, passing an attractive manor house – King's Manor.

YAVERLAND (G)

The heart of the hamlet is the magnificent manor house, built by Jermyn Richards on the site of an earlier house, occupied for many years by the Russell family (later to become the Dukes of Bedford). It was Sir William Russell who, in the late 13th century, had the causeway and bridge built linking Bembridge and Yaverland to the rest of the Island. Before this 'Bembridge Isle' was often cut off by floods.

Jermyn Richards was a Welsh brewer who made his money supplying beer to the ships in Brading Haven or at anchor in St Helens Roads. The house he built was originally rectangular, and later the two wings were added with a date stone of 1620. The house can be seen from the road and is one of the finest manor houses on the Island, with a magnificent hall.

Close by is the Church of St John the Baptist, once a chapel to the manor. On the wall to the left of the doorway is a medieval scratch dial, put there in the days before clocks were common to ensure that the church bell was rung at the correct time. Inside the church a superb Norman arch provides an entry to the chancel. The church was

ABOVE *Yaverland, the Church of St John the Baptist, showing the Norman arch leading into the chancel.*

UPPER RIGHT & RIGHT *Yaverland. Two views of the Church of St John the Baptist. The engraving shows the manor house behind, and the photograph the result of considerable 19th century restoration to the church.*

considerably restored in the 19th century.

Along the road to Sandown are several cottages that go to make up the rest of the hamlet.

On the Down behind Yaverland is Bembridge Fort, built 1862-67 as part of the extensive defence system against possible invasion by French forces landing at Bembridge or in Whitecliff Bay. The fort was manned during both World Wars, in the latter serving as an anti-aircraft command post and H.Q. for the local Home Guard. Today it belongs to the National Trust, but is not open to the public.

Right at the end of the headland are the remains of Culver Battery which was completed in 1906 to defend the sea approaches to Portsmouth. Between the World Wars secret experiments were carried out with different types of military equipment. All guns were removed in 1956 and the site is now under the care of the National Trust.

The road linking the two sites provide beautiful views to the north across St Helens and Bembridge, and to the south right across Sandown Bay to Luccombe.

The National Trust

The National Trust owns and maintains more than 4,000 acres of beautiful countryside and 17 miles of fine coastline on the Isle of Wight, allowing visitors and residents alike access to areas ranging from the Needles headland to rolling ownland and to Culver Cliff.

In West Wight there are several fine areas of Trust-owned land to enjoy, including Headon Warren, the largest area of heathland on the Island. A walk here offers fine views of the western Solent and beyond to the New Forest. Another route, covering Compton Down and Compton Bay, is rich in wildlife, especially wild flowers and butterflies. Compton Bay also boasts one of the Island's finest beaches.

The East Wight also has several excellent walks, including an area of ancient woodland known as Borthwood Copse, which can be enjoyed all the year round. Also recommended is Bembridge and Culver Down, where the route passes a Victorian fort (not open to the public) and includes a stretch of down that gives views of the eastern Solent to the north and over Sandown Bay to the south. At the end of the headland lie the remains of Culver Battery, a Second World War defence.

The National Trust also owns and maintains a number of the Island's important historic buildings. Mottistone Manor House is an attractive 15th/16th century building set in a splendid garden. The manor was once owned by the Cheke family, one of whom, Sir John, was tutor to Edward VI. In around 1700 the west end of the house was engulfed by the subsidence of an earth bank at the rear of the house. After this it was occupied by tenant farmers. In 1861 the house and estate was bought by Charles

The view across Freshwater Bay to Tennyson Down which is managed by the National Trust.

The view from St. Catherine's Down, owned by the National Trust, across the Back of the Wight to High Down.

Seely, a wealthy Nottinghamshire colliery owner who had retired to the Island. His grandson, Jack Seely, became the first Lord Mottistone. It was his son, an architect, who restored the house and, in 1963, bequeathed most of the estate to the Trust. The gardens are now open from spring to autumn, but the house is only open on August Bank Holiday.

A much smaller building under the control of the Trust is Newtown Town Hall. The building seen today is 18th century on a 17th century plinth and is one of few remaining indicators to Newtown's past as an important port. By the early 1930s the building was in a bad state of repair and the local landlord presented it to the Trust. The restoration, in 1935, was funded by the 'Ferguson Gang', an anonymous group known by names such as Sister Agatha, The Nark, and Red Biddy. The group successfully raised money to save several old buildings in England. Clearly they had a sense of drama as they would anonymously deliver sacks full of cash to the National Trust's offices.

The Needles Old Battery is also well worth a visit. Originally built in 1860 to guard against the threat of invasion by the French, it was still in use, as a rocket testing site, until the 1960s. Two original gun barrels survive on the parade ground where you can also find the entrance to a long tunnel, which leads to a searchlight position that has wonderful views out to sea. For those not interested in military history, there are stunning views of the Needles with the lighthouse at the sea end and, farther on, across to the mainland.

On the East Wight is Bembridge Windmill, a very different building that is also in the Trust's care. Built in the mid 18th century it was restored in the 1930s and taken on by the Trust in 1962. The visitor now has the chance to see not only the building but much of the machinery that was used in its day-to-day life.

Newtown Town Hall is in the care of the Trust and is open to the public.

Museums

The rich and varied history of the Isle of Wight is told at 14 museums and heritage centres dotted around the Island, ranging from the Museum of Island History to the Dinosaur Farm Museum. All have something to offer, either for historians engaged in serious study or families seeking a pleasant day out.

The oldest of the Island museums is the **Carisbrooke Castle Museum**, which was founded by Princess Beatrice, the youngest child of Queen Victoria, more than 100 years ago. Today, the main displays relate to the history of the castle, local social history and the story of the imprisonment of Charles I at the castle. It is well worth a visit, especially if combined with a visit to the buildings.

A much more modern establishment is the **Museum of Island History**, which is in High Street, Newport. Still developing and with plans for further expansion, the museum has a good mixture of interactive displays, exhibits of all aspects of Island history and a small art gallery which has paintings of local scenes.

For those interested in the Island's Roman past there are Roman villas at both Brading and

The museum in Carisbrooke Castle is over 100 years old and is a must for anybody visiting the Castle.

Newport. **Brading Roman Villa** is famous for its remarkable mosaics, whilst the baths and hypocaust system at **Newport Roman Villa** are amongst the best preserved in Britain.

Naturally, the Isle of Wight's world renown in the world of fossils and dinosaurs is not ignored. The **Dinosaur Farm Museum** is near Brighstone in the south and here visitors can talk to experts working on the conservation of recently discovered fossilised bones. There is also **Dinosaur Isle** at Sandown, which features interactive displays, dinosaur skeletons and a large fossil collection, all housed in a distinctive modern building.

As might be expected on an island there are a

Exhibits at the Newport Roman villa. Together with the villa at Brading, the two Roman villas on the Island reflect different aspects of Roman life, and are well worth visiting.

The Isle of Wight Bus Museum, Newport, is one of several museums on the Island devoted to transport.

A beautifully restored river launch housed in the Classic Boat Museum, Newport.

Julia Margaret Cameron, from the painting by George Frederic Watts. The Dimbola Lodge Museum at Freshwater Bay has a permanent display of her photographs.

number of places dedicated to maritime history. The **Cowes Maritime Museum** is attached to the local library and has displays of models and paintings of local maritime scenes. In Cowes High Street is **Sir Max Aitken Museum**, housed in the old Ratsey's sail loft. Here, the visitor can see nautical instruments, paintings and artefacts collected by Aitken, a keen yachtsman and son of Lord Beaverbrook, the newspaper magnate.

Across the river, in Clarence Road, is **East Cowes Heritage Centre**. This volunteer-run centre has regular displays related to various aspects of local history. The **Shipwreck Centre**, formerly at Bembridge, now at Arreton Barns, features hundreds of objects from the collection of deep-sea diver, Martin Woodward. These range from Spanish 'pieces of eight' to objects from the Second World War. The **Bembridge Heritage Centre** has an exhibition of past and present village life within a former Victorian school.

Museums dealing with transport include the **Isle of Wight Bus Museum** at Riverside, Newport, which has a good selection of vehicles dating from 1890 to the present day. Nearby is the **Classic Boat Museum** with a fine collection of restored classic boats dating back to the 19th century. At Northwood, near Cowes, the **Military History Museum** has a selection of tanks, armoured cars and artillery, all on display undercover, as well as

the opportunity to see restoration being carried out.

At Freshwater Bay, in the western part of the Island, is **Dimbola Lodge Museum**, the former home of the pioneering Victorian photographer Julia Margaret Cameron. The museum is chiefly dedicated to her life and work but also has regular photographic exhibitions.

A museum which is different, but appeals to many and is well-worth visiting, is the **Lilliput Antique Doll and Toy Museum**, whose fine collection numbers over 2,000 exhibits.

This is just a cross-section of what can be seen on the Island. Several towns and villages now have their own heritage societies and centres.

A model of a Polacanthus in the Dinosaur Isle Museum, Sandown.

Acknowledgements

I am very grateful to my daughter Marion and her husband Richard Whitehead for sorting out the manuscript and putting it on disc. My thanks also to David Burnett, my publisher, for editing the text. A special thank you to my wife for her patience and support.

To the following I give my thanks for freely giving of their time and specialist knowledge, and for making an important contribution to this book: Marion Brinton for 'Local Building Tradition', Martin Munt for 'A Brief Geological History', and Bill Shepard for 'A Naturalist's Paradise'.

I would like to thank the following for their help with the text: Fay Brown, Lord Mottistone, Richard Smout, Charles Taylor, David Tomalin, Leslie Turner, Clifford Webster and Isle of Wight Tourism.

A special debt is owed to Don French and David Yendall for their help with the illustrations, but I would also like to thank the following: Graham Bowler (Isle of Wight Bus Museum), Roger George Clark, Jo Cowan (Brading Roman Villa), Alison Cullingford (J.B. Priestley Library, The University of Bradford), Khol Dieu (Octopus Publishing Group), Sandra Fearon and David Cheek (GKN Aerospace), Jack and Johanna Jones, Anthony Kersting, Chris Mawson (Simmons Aerofilms Ltd), Julie Mearns (Department of Prehistory and Europe, British Museum), Martin Munt, Peter Pusey (Dinosaur Isle), Alyson Rogers and Nigel Wilkins (English Heritage), Celia Sterne (English Heritage Photographic Library), Helen Trompeteler (The National Portrait Gallery), Colin Varndell, Corina Westwood and John Fletcher (Isle of Wight Museums Service),

I am also grateful to Christopher Chaplin for drawing the geology map and the town maps.

I would finally like to thank the following for allowing the reproduction of illustrations in their possession or for which they hold the copyright: Brading Roman Villa, 6 centre; Roy Brinton, copyright page, 19 top, 22, 23 top, 24 top, 28 centre, 40 top, 41, 42, 43, 44, 47 left, 49 bottom, 53, 54 bottom right, 64 top left, 68, 69 top, 71 top, 72 centre, 74 both, 76 bottom, 78 top, 82 top & bottom, 85, 87 all, 88 all, 90 centre, 91 bottom, 100 bottom, 103 top, 104 both, 105 bottom, 106 top & bottom left, 107 both, 111 bottom left, 112 top, 113 top & bottom, 114 bottom, 115 bottom left, 116 bottom, 117 both, 122 bottom; The British Museum, 12 top right; Roger George Clark, 45 top & bottom, 46 top right, 47 top right, 99 top left & right; © Crown Copyright. Cartography by Philip's. © Philip's, an imprint of the Octopus Publishing Group Ltd, 2005, colour map; © Crown copyright. NMR, 59 top right; Dinosaur Isle Museum, Sandown, 7 bottom; The Dovecote Press, 12 top left, 21 top right & bottom, 23 centre, 26 top left, 34 top, 39 top, 54 bottom left, 55 top, 56 top right, 61 bottom right, 67 bottom, 69 bottom, 70 centre, 77 top left, 92 top left, 109 bottom, 115 top left, 122 top right; English Heritage Photographic Library, 110; Reproduced by permission of English Heritage.NMR, 14 bottom, 30 top, 59 top left, 62 top, 93 centre, 102 bottom; Don French, title page, 6 bottom, 7 top, 8, 9, 11 top, 11 bottom left, 12 bottom, 14 top, 15 bottom, 25 both, 26 bottom, 27 centre, 28 top, 29 top left, 31 bottom, 32 bottom, 34 bottom, 35 both, 36, 37 bottom, 40 bottom right, 45 centre, 46 bottom, 47 bottom, 48 bottom, 52 bottom, 55 centre, 56 bottom, 57 both, 59 bottom, 60 top right & bottom, 64 top right, 70 top, 72 bottom, 76 top, 77 top right & bottom left & right, 79 both, 81 bottom, 84 top, centre & bottom left, 89, 90 top, 91 top, 92 bottom both, 94, 99 bottom right, 101 both, 102 top, 103 bottom, 105 top, 114 top, 118 top, 119 top & bottom, 120 top & center, 121 bottom, 125 top; GKN Aerospace, 38 top & bottom left, 81 top; The Isle of Wight Bus Museum, 125 bottom right; Isle of Wight Museum Services, 33 right, 125 bottom left, 126 bottom; Jack & Johanna Jones, 9 top, 10 left, 10 right, 10 centre, 13 both, 14 centre, 17 top right, 28 bottom, 29 top right, 30 bottom, 33 left, 40 bottom left, 55 bottom, 61 bottom left, 62 centre, bottom left & right, 70 bottom, 72 top right, 80 top left, 100 top right, 119 centre, 120 bottom, 121 top; A.F. Kersting, 6 top, 11 bottom right, 16, 17, top left, 19 bottom, 20 top & centre, 29 bottom, 38 right, 60 top left, 95, 97 top, 108 both, 109 top, 111 top & bottom right, 113 centre, 122 top left; Lord Mottistone, 54 top; Martin Munt, 51; NMR\Knight Frank, 26 top right, 27 top; NMR © George Nuttall, 109 centre; National Portrait Gallery, London, 126 top right; J.B. Priestley Library, University of Bradford, 118 bottom; Simmons Aerofilms Ltd, 37 top; Thearle photography, 75; Colin Varndell, 67 top; David Yendall, 15 top, 17 bottom, 18 both, 20 bottom, 21 top left, 24 centre, 31 top & center, 32 top, 39 bottom, 46 top left, 48 top, 49 top, 52 top, 56 top left, 61 top, 63, 64 bottom, 65, 66, 71 bottom, 72 top left, 73 all four, 78 bottom, 80 top right, 82 centre, 83 both, 84 bottom right, 90 bottom, 92 top right, 93 top & bottom, 96, 97 bottom left & right, 98 both, 99 bottom left, 100 top left, 105 centre, 106 bottom right, 112 centre & bottom, 115 top right & bottom right, 116 top, 123, 124 both, 126 top left.

A final debt is owed to Don French for providing all the photographs reproduced in the colour section, and all those on the front and back cover.

The Lists

Contents

These are not lists of what you can see on the Isle of Wight, but lists of the places which have opening times or events which occur at certain times of the year. Further descriptions of most of them can be found under their entry in the Gazetteer, where their map reference letter is also given. Landscapes, villages and towns are not included, but are found in the Gazetteer, and in some cases (eg. National Trust) they are also mentioned in the various double page spread sections on specific subjects. In all cases their map reference letter is given at the start of their entry in the Gazetteer.

Unless otherwise stated the months in the Lists are complete, e.g. March-Sept means March 1st to September 30th. All the information given was correct when this edition of the Guide went to press, but phone numbers are given wherever possible and we would suggest you check opening times in the winter or if you are making a long journey. A lot of work has gone into the Lists but we have had to rely on advance information, some of which may prove inaccurate. Tourist Information Offices are a good standby and will be happy to help: all of them are shown on the town maps and phone numbers are given in the Lists. We apologize for any mistakes or omissions.

Price Guide: A: less than £1, B: less than £3, C: less than £5, D: £5 and over. The key gives the price of a single adult ticket, but most places give reductions for children and Old Age Pensioners, and some offer family tickets. Please remember that not all the places charge admission.

Animals, Birds, Fishes and Butterflies

Amazon World Zoo Park, Watery Lane, Arreton. Exotic animal park. All year daily from 10am. Price D. 01983 867122.

Butterfly World, Wootton Bridge. Indoor gardens with exotic flying butterflies. April-Oct daily from 10am. Price D. 01983 883430.

Colman's Animal Farm, Porchfield. Feed and cuddle friendly animals. Mid March-Oct Tues-Sun from 10am. Price D. 01983 522831.

Seaview Wildlife Encounter, Springvale, Seaview. Award winning wildlife park. Mid March-Sept daily from 10am. Price D. 01983 612261.

Isle of Wight Donkey Sanctuary, Lower Winstone Farm, Wroxall. Home of over 200 donkeys. May-Oct daily from 10.30am. Free admission. 01983 852693.

Isle of Wight Owl & Falconry Centre, Wroxall, Ventnor. Flying displays of birds of prey. Mid Feb-Oct daily from 10am. Price C. 01983 852484.

Isle of Wight Zoo, Yaverland, Sandown. Home of the tiger and rare and endangered species. Mid Feb-Oct daily from 10am. Price D. 01983 403883.

Brickfields Horse Country, Newnham Road, Binstead. Horses - from Shires to miniature Shetland. All year daily from 10am. Price D. 01983 566801.

Fort Victoria Marine Aquarium, Fort Victoria, Yarmouth. Discover many strange inhabitants of our sea and shore. April-Oct daily from 10am. Price B. 01983 760283.

Annual Events

May: Isle of Wight Walking Festival.
Early June: Yarmouth Old Gaffers Festival.
Mid-June: Round the Island Yacht Race.
End July: Mottistone Jazz Festival.
Early August: Skandia Cowes Week.

Mid-August: Isle of Wight County Show.
Late August: Garlic Festival, Newchurch.
August Bank Holiday week-end: Grand Island Steam Show, Havenstreet.
Mid-September: Isle of Wight Cycling Festival.

Castles and Forts

Carisbrooke Castle, Newport (English Heritage). Motte and Bailey castle where Charles I was imprisoned. All year daily, summer 10am-5pm, winter 10am-4pm. Price D. 01983 522107.

Yarmouth Castle, Yarmouth (English Heritage). One of Henry VIII's coastal defences. April-Sept Sun-Thurs 11am-4pm. Price B. 01983 760678.

Needles Old Battery, West High Down, Alum Bay (National Trust). 19th century coastal fort. April-Oct Sat-Thurs. Daily July-Aug 10.30am-5pm. Price C. 01983 754772.

Churches

As far as the author is aware, churches are either open or the keys can be borrowed from an address indicated in the church porch.

Gardens

Afton Park Nursery, Orchard and Gardens, Newport Road, Freshwater Bay. Six acres of meadow, gardens and orchard. March-Oct Mon-Sat 9.30am-5pm. Sun 10.30am-4.30pm. Free admission. 01983 755774.

Morton Manor House Gardens, Brading. Beautiful house set in award winning gardens. Easter-Oct Sun-Fri 10am-5.30pm. Price C. 01983 406168.

Mottistone Manor Garden, Mottistone. Tranquil garden with colourful borders adjoining the Manor House. Late March-Oct Sun-Thurs 11am-5.30pm. Price C. 01983 741302.

Ventnor Botanic Gardens, Undercliff Drive, Ventnor. 22 acres of gardens with rare and exotic species. All year daily 10am-5pm (6pm in high season). Free admission. 01983 855397.

Houses

Appuldurcombe House, Wroxall (English Heritage). Partially restored shell of 18th century house. Daily Mar-Oct 10am-3pm, May-Sept 10am-5pm. Price B. 01983 852484.

Arreton Manor House, Arreton. One of the most important manor houses on the Island. April-Oct 10am-5pm (closed Sat). Gardens and tearoom. House open Wed & Sun only. Price B. 01983 522604.

Morton Manor House, Brading. Historic family house set in beautiful gardens. Easter-Oct 10am-5.30pm Sun-Fri (closed Sat). Price C. 01983 406168.

Mottistone Manor House, Mottistone. Very interesting house and history. August Bank Holiday Monday only. (See GARDENS for opening of grounds). 01983 741302.

Nunwell House and Gardens, Coach Lane, Brading. Fine country house with a great history. July-Aug Mon-Wed 1pm-5pm. Price C. 01983 407240.

Osborne House, East Cowes (English Heritage). The country home of Queen Victoria and Prince Albert. Daily April-Sept 10am-6pm, Oct 10am-5pm Sun-Thurs. Price D. 01983 200022.

Mills

Bembridge Windmill, Mill Lane, Bembridge (National Trust). The Island's only surviving windmill. End March-Oct 10am-4.30pm Sun-Fri. July & Aug daily. Price B. 01983 873945.

Calbourne Watermill, Calbourne, Newport. 17th century working watermill. Price D. End March-Oct 10am-5pm daily. 01983 531227.

Museums

Bembridge Heritage Centre, Church Road, Bembridge. Fascinating exhibition of past and present village life. Easter-mid-Oct Mon, Wed, Fri 10am-4pm. Sat 10am-noon. Price B. Enquiries 01983 874218.

Brighstone Village Museum, Brighstone. Small museum of Victorian village life. Open all year except 25 Dec-28 Dec & 1 Jan. Times vary. Free admission. 01983 740689.

Carisbrooke Castle Museum, Newport. The Island's history plus objects connected with Charles I. See entry in 'Castles and Forts' for opening times and prices. 01983 523112.

Classic Boat Museum, Newport Harbour, Newport. Collection of lovingly restored classic boats. Open daily April-Oct. Price C. 01983 533493.

Cowes Maritime Museum, Beckford Road, Cowes. Exhibition of paintings and models depicting local maritime history. All year 9.30am-5.30pm Mon, Tues & Fri. Wed 11am-7pm. Sat 9.30am-4.30pm. Closed Thurs, Sun & Bank Holidays. Free admission. 01983 823433.

Dimbola Lodge Museum, Terrace Lane, Freshwater Bay. Museum and galleries in the home of the famous Victorian photographer, Margaret Cameron. All year 10am-5pm Tues-Sun. Every day during school holidays. Price C. 01983 756814.

Dinosaur Farm Museum, Brighstone. View experts working on the conservation of dinosaur bones. Open April-Oct 10am-5pm Sun, Tues & Thurs. Daily mid-July-Aug. Price C. 01983 740844.

Dinosaur Isle, Culver Parade, Sandown. View fleshed out dinosaurs, dinosaur skeletons & fossils. Open all year daily April-Sept 10am-6pm; Oct 10am-5pm; Nov-Mar 10am-4pm. Price C. 01983 404344.

Isle of Wight Bus & Coach Museum, The Quay, Newport. Collection of vehicles and passenger memorabilia from 1890. Open mid-April-Sept, Sun, Tues, Wed & Thurs Daily throughout school summer holidays. Tues only in Oct. The Annual Autumn Running is usually on a Sunday in October. 10.30am-4pm. Price C. 01983 533352.

Isle of Wight Military History Museum, Northwood. All weather attraction of tanks, armoured cars and artillery. Open 10am-5pm daily. Price C. 01983 527411.

Lilliput Antique Doll and Toy Museum, High St., Brading. Fine collection of antique dolls, toys and rare playthings. Open daily 10am-5pm except 25 Dec. Price B. 01983 407231.

Museum of Island History, Guildhall, High Street, Newport. Story of the Island from the past to the present day. Open all year Mon-Sat 10am-5pm. Sun 11am-3.30pm. Price B. 01983 823366/823847.

Sir Max Aitken Museum, High Street, Cowes. Housed in old sailmakers loft, this museum exhibits the unique collection of Sir Max Aitken's nautical instruments, paintings etc. Open May-Oct Tues-Sat 10am-4pm. Price A. 01983 295144.

Jacob's Yard, Shipwreck Centre, Arreton Barns Craft Village, Arreton. Devoted to local maritime heritage as well as a brewery, steam engines etc. Open daily. 01983 539361.

Nature Reserves and Country Parks

The Island is very fortunate in having so many nature reserves kept by the I.W. Council and other charitable trusts. Below is a selection which the public can enjoy.

Afton Marches, Freshwater Bay. 37 acres which covers several types of wetland habitat, home of water voles, various butterflies and breeding birds such as warblers.

Alverstone Mead, south east of Alverstone (Wight Nature Fund). 43 acres of low-lying grasslands, hay meadows, ditches and woodland. A wide range of wild flowers can be enjoyed. Several public footpaths across the reserve.

Arreton Down, Downend, Arreton (Hampshire & I.W. Wildlife Trust). Nearly 74 acres of open chalk downland with fine views south across the Arreton Valley.

Brading Down, eastern end of the central ridge of chalk downs and is crossed by the main Newport to Brading road. Walkers can enjoy the large area of open downland (80 acres). Plenty of wildlife. There are car parks bordering the main road.

Brading Reserve, north east of Brading (R.S.P.B.). At one time the area was covered by sea water at high tide. In the 19th century it was drained and became meadow land. The 617 acres are the home of many birds including redshanks and lapwings. Car parking near Brading Church.

Compton Down, east of Freshwater Bay, north of the Military Road (National Trust). Nearly 3 miles of open downland rich in wildlife especially butterflies and wild flowers. There are views north across the Island and to the south out to sea. Car park at Freshwater Bay.

Dodnor Creek, about a mile north of Newport along the cycle way to Cowes. Nearly 22 acres of woodland and millpond. Spring flowers, such as primroses, bugle and narrow leaved lugwort, are to be found. All year round there are birds to be enjoyed.

Golden Hill, south of the A3054, between Yarmouth and Colwell. 50 acres of land surrounding a Victorian fort. The soil produces a selection of chalk loving plants. Car park.

Nansen Hill, eastern end of the Ventnor Downs between Bonchurch and Luccombe. 11½ acres of open downland. Fine chalk grassland with a range of flowers. This hill was obtained in 1932 by J.H. Whitehouse, Warden of Bembridge School. He named it in memory of Dr. Fridtjo Nansen (1861-1930), a Norwegian explorer who promoted 'peace and friendship' between nations. Car park opposite entrance gate on the Ventnor to Shanklin road.

Rew Down, western side of Ventnor. 29 acres of downland which in the spring has a carpet of bluebells and cowslips.

Robin Hill Country Park, Downend, Arreton. 80 acres of woodland and downs with rides and attractions for all ages. Open daily April-Oct 10am-5pm. Aug 10am-6pm. Price D. 01983 730052.

Fort Victoria Country Park, Yarmouth. 50 acres of woodland centred around a Victorian fort. Free admission. 01983 823893.

Tourist Information Centres

Cowes. Fountain Quay. April-Oct Mon-Sat 9.30am-5.30pm. Sunday 10am-4pm. Winter - Reduced opening hours.

Newport. The Guildhall, High Street. All year Mon-Sat 9.30am-5.30pm. Sunday 10am-4pm.

Ryde. Western Esplanade. April-Oct Mon-Sat 9.30am-5.30pm. Sunday April-June, Sept & Oct 10am-4pm, July & Aug 9.30am-4.30pm. Winter - Reduced opening hours.

Sandown. 8, High Street. April-Oct Mon-Sat 9.30am-5.30pm. Sunday April-June, Sept & Oct 10am-4pm, July & Aug 9.30am-4.30pm. Winter - Reduced opening hours.

Shanklin. 67 High Street. April-Oct Mon-Sat 9.30am-5.30pm. Sunday April-June, Sept & Oct 10am-4pm, July & Aug 9.30am-4.30pm. Winter - Reduced opening hours.

Ventnor. Salisbury Gardens, Dudley Road. April-Oct Mon-Sat 9.30am-4.30pm. Winter - Reduced opening hours.

Yarmouth. The Quay. April-Oct Mon-Sat 9.30am-5.30pm. Sunday April-June, Sept & Oct 10am-4pm, July & Aug 9.30am-4.30pm. Winter - Reduced opening hours.

For general information on the Island call 01983 813818.

For accommodation on the Island call 01983 813813.

Miscellaneous

Adgestone Vineyard, Adgestone. Vineyard and working winery plus wine tasting. Open all year 10am-5.30 pm in season. Free admission. Charge for tours. 01983 402503.

Arreton Barns Craft Village, Arreton. Craft village with a pub and a herbal craft shop. Open daily. 01983 528353/539361.

Blackgang Chine, Chale. Fantasy attractions and heritage exhibitions plus boat water slide and pirate fort. Open daily April-Oct 10am-5pm, August 10am-10pm. 01983 730052.

Brading Experience, 46 High Street, Brading. Wax works, chamber of horrors, animal world and other attractions. Open daily 10am-5pm. Price D. 01983 407286.

Brading Roman Villa, Old Morton Road, Brading. New £3 million exhibition and visitor centre covering some of the finest mosaics in England. Open daily all year except Christmas week 9.30am-6pm. Price C. 01983 406223.

Chessell Pottery Barns, Chessel, Calbourne. Decorate your own pottery and watch potters at work. Open daily Easter-Oct 9.30am-5.30pm. 01983 531248.

Coastal Visitors Centre, Salisbury Gardens, Dudley Rd., Ventnor. Exhibition of all aspects of the local coast line. Open all year Mon-Fri 9.30am-5pm, Saturdays 9.30am-4.30pm. Price A. 01983 855400.

Fort Victoria Model Railway, Fort Victoria, Yarmouth. One of the largest model railways. Open daily Easter-Sept. Weekends and half term in Oct. Price C. 01983 761553.

Garlic Farm, Mersley Lane, Newchurch. Home of I.W. Garlic - Taste a large range of flavours. Open Mon-Sat 9.30am-5pm. Sun 10am-1pm. July-Sept Sun 10am-5pm. Free admission. 01983 865378.

Island Brass Rubbing Centre, The Coach House, St. George's Church, Arreton. Craft centre for facsimile brasses and brass rubbings. Open Easter-Oct Mon-Sat 10am-5pm. Sun 12.30pm-5pm. Free admission. 01983 527553.

Island Planetarium and Astronomy Centre, Fort Victoria, Yarmouth. Planetarium theatre and space exhibition with multimedia shows. Shows 10.30am-5pm weekdays in school holidays. Phone to check other times. Price C. 0800 1958295.

Island Speedway, Smallbrook Stadium, Ashey Road, Ryde. Premier League 500cc motorcycle speedway. Open 6pm every Tues April-Oct and Thurs in Aug. Price D. 01983 811180.

Isle of Wight Lavender, Staplehurst Grange, Staplers Road, Newport. Producers of highest quality lavender and natural cosmetics. Tearoom. Open Mon-Sat 10am-5pm and Sun 10am-4pm. Closed Wed Oct-end Feb. Free admission. 01983 825272.

Isle of Wight Pearl, Chilton Chine, Military Road, Brighstone. Display of over 32,000 pieces of jewellery. Open all year Mon-Sat from 10am. Sun 10.30am-4.30pm. Free admission. 01983 740352.

Isle of Wight Steam Railway, Havenstreet. Genuine vintage train ride - 10 mile round trip. Trains operate selected days April-Oct, daily operation June-mid-September. Price D. 01983 884343.

Isle of Wight Studio Glass, Old Park, St. Lawrence. Watch the production of the fascinating craft of glass making. Open Mon-Fri 9am-4.30pm. Sat summer only. 01983 853526.

L.A. Bowl, The Pavilion, Esplanade, Ryde. Modern 22 lane tenpin bowling centre. Open daily all year 10am till late. Prices vary. 0808 1085353.

An **R.N.L.I. lifeboat** can be seen at the Quay in Yarmouth Harbour. Another is stationed at Bembridge in a building at the end of the pier. This station is sometimes opened to the public during the summer.

Model Village, High Street, Godshill. Beautiful model village depicting Godshill and Shanklin old villages as they were in yesteryear. Open daily March-Dec from 10am. Price C. 01983 840270.

Needles Park, Alum Bay. A very popular attraction which includes glass making, sweet manufacturing and a spectacular chairlift to the beach. Open Easter-Oct daily 10am-5pm. Free entry - attractions individually charged. 0870 4580022.

Newport Roman Villa, Cypress Road, Newport. Well preserved remains of Romano British farmhouse. Open April-Oct Mon-Sat 10am-4.30pm. Sun July & Aug only noon-4pm. Price B. 01983 529720.

Newtown Old Town Hall, Newtown (National Trust). 17th century town hall - only evidence of the one-time importance of this town, also exhibitions. Open April-Oct Sun, Mon & Wed 2pm-5pm. July & Aug Sun-Thurs 2pm-5pm. Price B. 01983 531785.

Planet Ice, Quay Road, Ryde. Ice rink open all year. Open daily 10am-4.30pm plus Mon 8pm-10pm. Disco Wed, Fri and Sat evenings. 01983 615155.

Quay Arts, Sea Street, Newport. Four galleries plus music, theatre and craft workshops. Open all year Mon-Sat 10am-4pm. Free for galleries. 01983 822490.

Rosemary Vineyard, Smallbrook Lane, Ryde. Stroll round the vineyard - guided or unguided tours, plus free wine tasting. Open all year Easter-Oct Mon-Sat 10am-6pm. Sun 11am-4pm. Closed Sun Jan & Feb. 01983 811084.

Sandown Pier, Esplanade, Sandown. Have a day of fun with adventure golf, Superbowl, dodgems and more attractions. Open every day summer 9am-11pm, winter 9am-10pm. Free admission to pier. 01983 404122.

Shanklin Chine, Old Village, Shanklin. Beautiful and historic gorge with dramatic waterfalls, also an annual exhibition. Open April-Oct daily 10am-5pm. June-Mid-Sept 10am-10pm when floodlit. Price C. 01983 866432.

St. Catherine's Lighthouse, Niton. Visitors are offered guided tours. For opening hours check with Tourist Information Centres. Price B. 01983 855069.

St Thomas's Heritage Centre, St. Thomas's St., Ryde. The restored former church now houses exhibitions on local history and conservation techniques used to restore historic buildings. Open Mon-Fri during office hours. Free admission.

Waltzing Waters, Westridge Centre, Brading Road, Ryde. Water, light and music spectacular presented indoors. Contact for times. Price C. 01983 811333.